CLINT EASTWOOD

'I was never the guy the press agents figured should be on the cover of this or that magazine, never the recipient of the big, glamorous studio push they gave upcoming actors in the old days. I've never been the darling of any particular group, but somehow – somehow – I got there.' Clint Eastwood doesn't pretend to have all the answers. Very like *The Man With No Name*, conceived in 1964 on a sandswept desert in Spain, he's got a set of rules that work for him, and they're the ones he plans on sticking to. He's perfectly satisfied by the way things have worked out, not regretting for a minute the bad times in the past that threatened to keep him hanging in on the bit-part lists indefinitely.

Clint Eastwood

The Man Behind the Myth

Patrick Agan

CORONET BOOKS
Hodder and Stoughton

Copyright © 1975 by Patrick Agan

First published in Great Britain
1977 by Robert Hale Limited

Coronet edition 1978
Second impression 1978

British Library C. I. P.
Agan, Patrick
  Clint Eastwood.
  1. Eastwood, Clint
  2. Moving-picture actors and actresses – United
     States – Biography
  I. Title
     791.43'028'0924   PN2287.E37

ISBN 0–340–23090–8

Printed and bound in Great Britain for
Hodder and Stoughton Paperbacks, a
division of Hodder and Stoughton Ltd.,
Mill Road, Dunton Green, Sevenoaks,
Kent (Editorial Office: 47 Bedford
Square, London, WC1 3DP) by
Cox & Wyman Ltd, London, Reading and Fakenham

DEDICATION

This book is dedicated to the American Film Institute for its
invaluable work in preserving the great films of our time and
fostering new talent to carry on Hollywood's cinematic tradi-
tions. The A.F.I. and its guiding spirit Charlton Heston recognise that film is the authentic art form of the twentieth century,
and their cause deserves the support of moviegoers everywhere.

And to my parents Eugene and Marjorie Agan for their help
and encouragement, this book is a minor way of saying thank
you.

In the words of Clint Eastwood:

'Hollywood is a strange place. Everyone is looking for a formula. One year it's two guys on a motorcycle, the next it's a girl dying of cancer. For years I bummed around trying to get a job and it was the same old story – my voice was too soft, my teeth needed capping, I squinted too much, I was too tall. All that tearing down of my ego, it was bound to turn me into either a better person or a bastard . . .'

Contents

The Image of Eastwood — 9

The Western Myth and Clint Eastwood—The Man on the Screen Isn't an Eight-by-Ten Glossy! — 11

The Early Years — 28

The Army and Maggie Johnson — 37

How Did a Nice Boy like You Get in a Place like This? — 46

The *Rawhide* Years — 57

A Fistful of Dollars — 66

Hail the Reconquering Hero — 76

Back in Business with Siegel — 88

The Other Side of the Viewfinder—*Play Misty for Me* — 97

The Man with No Name Meets *Dirty Harry* — 106

Back in the Saddle—*Joe Kidd* and *High Plains Drifter* — 115

Hollywood's Newest Renaissance Man — 123

Dirty Harry Rides Again! — 130

Prognosis Positive — 140

Filmography — 151

The Image of Eastwood

Not since James Bond hit the movie screen like a thunderbolt in *Dr. No* has a character so hypnotised audiences by the millions as has The Man With No Name – otherwise known as Clint Eastwood. He's a phenomenon and a paradox in a time when even the biggest stars may have box-office flops. Clint's had only one flop in the years since he first loped across the screen in the gritty Spaghetti Western *A Fistful of Dollars*, and he's parlayed his unbeatable charisma into a top position, which guarantees he can write his own ticket at any movie studio in the world.

He's big, he's bad, and he's beautiful in a way no other star has ever been. He's as unique as a mountain man. He dominates a scene as forcefully as a lion cub in a cage full of housecats. To men, he's Super Dude. To women, he's Super Stud. He suggests a masculine directness more by mood and look than words, and everybody gets the message. He doesn't talk loudly but he's always heard.

Eastwood's films have grossed over a quarter of a billion dollars at the world's box office windows, and he's revolutionised the word hero. He's added to the myth of the Western hero – just as Mick Jagger has to rock and roll – making it live again by investing his screen characters with a realism that simultaneously shocks and tantalises. There's seldom a movie where Clint isn't battered and bloodied by the other side, but no matter how much punishment he takes, Eastwood always comes back for more, to the cheers of an audience more accustomed nowadays to seeing its heroes lose.

Spend A Night With Clint Eastwood has been a drive-in slogan for years now, usually playing his three Spaghetti Westerns for a night-long feast of blood, rape, pillage, lust and revenge. He hits the seven deadly sins one by one and knocks

9

them all into his special world of near respectability. He's a survivor first, a man second, although in the world of his films you can't be one without the other.

There's a cult surrounding Clint as a star, the likes of which hasn't been seen in decades. On screen he's basically always The Man With No Name but his movies are seldom defined by title – they're simply Clint Eastwood pictures, just as there once were Clark Gable pictures and Gary Cooper pictures.

Clint Eastwood is the first star since Paul Newman whom the public wants to grow with, and he's smart enough to know just what it takes to make them happy. He's every man's fantasy figure – a combination Superman and gas jockey rolled into a 6 ft. 4 in. flat-bellied piston of energy who has sparked a success story that's made him the number one box-office star in the world. He's called by many names and none, but there's no mistaking him – he's the man who shoots first and never gets around to the questions.

The Western Myth
and Clint Eastwood —
The Man on the Screen Isn't an
Eight-by-Ten Glossy!

The sun-scorched plains of Almeria, Spain have sweltered in their desert heat, virtually undisturbed, for centuries. It is dead land, just miles of sand and rocks, avoided by travellers and conquerors alike. The sun is an enduring enemy of the land, broiling it tirelessly year after year down through time. Only a foolish man would spend any more time under it than he had to, and only a careless one would openly welcome its fiery rays. Yet the tall, slightly bewhiskered man sitting calmly under the fiery ball looks neither foolish nor careless. His handsome features are thrust upward into the sun's brightest glare, and he greets it with a furrowed forehead, clenched mouth, and tightly-shut eyes; as if he wanted the intense heat to bake his thirty-four-year-old lines even deeper into his face. The natives give him a wide berth as he sits there in the summer of 1964, nodding back and forth between themselves of the loco American giant who speaks only when he's spoken to. Legends get born in the damnedest way!

Almeria was experiencing it's first prosperity in history. In those days of the early Sixties, movie producers had discovered the area's resemblance to the vast, empty reaches of the old American frontier – or what they remembered it looking like in the hundreds of Westerns they'd seen. Two small towns were rising up. One starkly compact and modern, the other a facsimile of those towns that once dotted the West. Both would be used by numerous movie production companies that would soon discover the area. This movie, which starred the lanky sunlover, was a foreshadowing of that blazing presence that would soon be lighting up movie screens around the world.

The company producing the film to be called *Per un Pugno di Dollari* (*A Fistful of Dollars*) was an Italian-West German-Spanish combine, and the film's director was a graduate of the spear-and-sandals epics of recent Italian movie fame named Sergio Leone. Its star was a laconic American named Clint Eastwood, known vaguely in Europe from the re-runs of his television series *Rawhide*. It was he who sat there under the searing sun, bending his frame up into its heat, letting it etch character into his face for the part he was to play – The Man With No Name.

Many of the film's interior shots were done at Rome's Cinecitta Studios. But the guts of it, the sense of space and isolation, the expanses of rocky terrain and wasteland, and the all-pervading sweat of it was generated in that forgotten corner of Spain, Almeria. The gun bursts that riddled the small, mythical town of San Miguel as The Man With No Name casually switched alliances would shortly ignite the box offices of Europe and the Orient, starting an avalanche of the made-in-Spain-by-Italians 'spaghetti westerns'. Working on a small budget, Leone didn't have extra dollars to spend on anything non-essential to his basic plot, a fact that shows on the screen in the close-ups of the primarily Italian cast.

The sullen machismo of Eastwood's role is immediately sensed as he rides slowly into town on a mule, slouch hat pulled down over narrowed eyes, a stubbly beard outlining his craggy face, punctuated by the unlit stub of a cigar clenched between his teeth. Surveying the scene for the first time and sensing the tensions beneath the surface, he remarks calmly to himself, 'There's money to be made in a place like this.' And silently, methodically he goes about getting it, aligning himself first with one side and then the other until they've all turned in on themselves, and, like a many-tailed scorpion, stung themselves to death. The super-cool essence of deadliness of the Man With No Name has been dismissed as a mere Italian fantasy, a satire on the Western hero. Yet millions have seen it as the incarnation of the figure who, a long time ago, made music with his guitar instead of his gun. *El Cigarillo*, as Clint Eastwood was nicknamed by the public who flocked to *A Fistful of Dollars*, shortly became the embodiment of every gunslinger, good *and* bad, who ever shot up a cardboard town in that ripest of fantasy gardens, the Western movie.

Eastwood arrived at a time when people were tired of talking, and action was the desire of everyone from college students to factory workers. His presence spelled the end of the Intellectual Westerns that had filled the screen with dialogue rather than bullets during the Fifties and early Sixties. Clint Eastwood became a personification of the times, a catchall of the doubts, fears, foibles and fantasies of every male with an identity crisis and every female who saw a male strength that was fast becoming as extinct as the dodo bird. The social and sexual revolutions of the Sixties had left a lot of potential victims without a cause or direction. The bluntness of Eastwood gave them something to look up to, even if at first it seemed nothing more than a larger-than-life lesson in mayhem. The drug culture picked up on him, too, with many of its converts seeing psychedelic origins in the trio of Italian Westerns that starred the ex-Rowdy Yates of television land. Budding law-and-order advocates idolised him, preferring his direct action to the more complicated machinery of the law. Eastwood movies offered something for everyone.

Western heroes have always been a measure of the times. In fact, cult heroes have proliferated in every society over the centuries, either legitimately, through the natural course of events, or they've been manufactured to fill the need for supermen that lurks in virtually every heart. Scandinavians have their Viking legends, the Japanese their inscrutably invincible Samurai, and Americans have the cowboy – perhaps the most believable hero of them all. That's the basic role Clint Eastwood has undertaken since *A Fistful of Dollars* catapulted him to superstardom.

The United States is a relatively young country, and we must pick our heroes from a period still relatively close to us. By definition, one requirement of a myth is that it be larger than life, and, recent history or not, our interpretation of how we won the West fills that bill perfectly. In our minds we see it as a vast unsettled territory peopled by savages who had to be conquered in order for us to grow as a nation. This subjugation, this epic conquering of a land so vast in so short a time – with all the accompanying emotions of pain, joy, sorrow, loneliness and, finally, death – has truly grand proportions. The conquest of the West has intrigued our imagination and that of the world ever since its completion just before the turn of the century. The final settling of the Western frontier came in 1893, according to historian Frederick Jackson Turner, and it was only five years later that we first began to glorify it with the Edison Company's short vignette *Cripple Creek Barroom*. The romance was on; soon thereafter Edwin S. Porter's *The Great Train Robbery* appeared – the first real *moving* picture with an integrated storyline that established a set of guidelines still acknowledged by Western moviemakers today.

That innovative movie was filmed in Dover, New Jersey, the birthstate of motion pictures, and Porter filmed it as a straight no-nonsense shoot out with cold-blooded bad guys and white-hatted good guys. Crude and primitive as it may appear today, the film has an astonishing realism, considering the time and the technical facilities available. Bronco Billy Anderson rode along then for ten years until, in 1914 in a picture called *The Bargain*, a new hero stuck his eagle-hooked nose up and grabbed the Western legend. This unlikely hero was a forty-four-year-old former stage actor named William S. Hart. For the next fifteen or so years Hart was the quintessential Westerner. His films were simple statements of right and wrong, extremely authentic in all details, but, curiously, his screen image was not absolutely all black or all white. Many people still remembered what the real West had been like and knew that his character's shades of grey were truer to its actual history. Unlike Clint Eastwood, though, Hart always had time to be reformed by a good woman. But until that happened in a film, he remained a silent, gaunt figure in an oversized hat, crouching dangerously behind a pair of six-guns.

As the times changed, so did public taste, and as the Twenties roared by and the Great Depression hit, there was a general longing for an idealised West where eternal truths were adhered to and life was simpler than it had suddenly turned out to be in those dark days of national crisis: a crisis that shattered many people's faith in the American system. Largely because of this attitude, the Western movie became escapist entertainment for the masses, and the movie house – including the grand palaces erected in the Twenties – became a place of refuge where people could put aside their real cares and flee back to what they now insisted was a better time. That was when the real saga of the West began to be forgotten, and in its place came the good guys, dozens of them, devised to give life to the lie the people wanted to see. Bill Hart's realism died, and in his place came a sterilised breed of man like Johnny Mack Brown, Hoot Gibson, Tim McCoy, Buck Jones and Ken Maynard – many of whom, we were led to believe, would rather sing a song than shoot a six-gun.

The Thirties were crammed with cowboy stars flourishing in hundreds of quickie B movies made to fill the constant appetite of the public for the misshaped myth that now covered the screens. Most were shot on studio backlots in a ten-day to two-week period and seldom were the top attraction of a studio, with the exception of Republic Pictures which specialised in them. Western stars were popular and often had huge followings, but there was something about them that precluded the adoration a Melvyn Douglas or a Cary Grant engendered. The story of the settling of the West fast became a Saturday afternoon popcorn seller, a story that was a complete fake.

The new Western hero was a snappy dresser, usually wearing some sort of 'personality' outfit replete with studs, fringe and a tooled saddle. In fact the only thing sartorially out of place was his constantly grizzled side-kick who eschewed the finery and offered a voice for reality with comments that boiled down to 'Let's quit fooling around and get cracking back to the way it really was – remember?' But the disgruntled voice was always laughed off by our hero as he snapped back the brim of his white hat and gently nudged his spangled horse into action. Of them all, perhaps the three most potent – visually, at least – were Tom Mix, always a vision in pristine white from head to toe; Hopalong Cassidy, (actually former silent screen star William Boyd) in black duds, but making up for that with silver accessories and a blindingly white horse (also with silver trim); and Roy Rogers, the acknowledged King of the Fringe. Rogers was perhaps the most durable of these legendary good guys and has kept his name and image alive through the years with shrewd merchandising. He is even contemplating a comeback. So inseparable were he and his faithful mount Trigger that when the horse succumbed to the inevitable, Rogers had him stuffed and displays him at his Western museum.

And let's not forget that other uniformed hero, Gene Autry, who invented the Singing Cowboy in 1935's *Tumbling Tumbleweeds* – an image that catapulted him to the top ten ranks of stars and also helped found one of show business's greatest financial empires. (But then the heroes have always been uniformed – even Clint Eastwood. As The Man With No Name, his scruffy appearance, high-lighted by the scroungy serape, dirty hat and bearded face, was just as appealing in the Sixties as cleanliness was in the earlier years.)

Every one of the good guys in the early days was pictured as a simon-pure Boy Scout – loyal, trustworthy, brave, out to get dog kickers, defend old ladies, and maybe once per picture, kiss a young woman.

Another, often overlooked reason for the Western film's 1930's clean-up was the inauguration of the Hays Office, a by now legendary bureau ruled over by Will Hays who for years was Hollywood's chief censor. Hays took his work seriously, and the result was a general emasculation in Hollywood with even its most virile figures suddenly turned into shy boys when – and if – they were ever shown in a lady's bedroom. If the bed contained a female, they couldn't even sit on its edge, and as for getting into it, not even fully clothed married people could do that. Hays' hopelessly unrealistic views on sex and how much of it the public should see only helped to further water down the once manly image of the American cowboy.

Handsome of face and manner, the new hero did know how to defend himself, but only did so if he'd been provoked beyond the limits of his gentlemanliness – and that's where the villains come in. You could always spot 'em. Wearing dark and dirty clothes and a stubble of beard, they rode a skinny horse, which they probably abused, *did* kick dogs when they got the chance, and were forever trying to get a kiss from the school-marm, or sheriff's daughter, or rancher's niece, or the Colonel's second cousin just visiting from Boston – the resident virgin, in any case. The ringleaders were of another stripe, well-oiled smoothies with expansive bellies and watch-chains to match, who called the shots from the backroom of a saloon or other equally naughty place, where, in their spare time, they un-doubtedly practised their perverted sexual habits, picked the wings off flies, and sharpened their amoral wits. They were always *smart* men, yet their intelligence was no match against Mr. Good with his handmade boots and silver bullets.

But black and white was what the audiences wanted and that's just what they got, a fact that led to some interesting Hollywood interpretations of history. Seedy outlaws like Billy the Kid, Frank and Jessie James and the Younger Brothers were whitewashed into virtual Robin Hoods of their times, and the strong-willed women who welded together the society of the Great Plains suffered an even more reprehensible fate. They became simpering ladies in spotless dresses with hairdos to match who, had they actually been so fragile, would have required so much attention that nothing would ever have got settled, let alone a new nation. On the other side were the bad girls who lived upstairs over the saloon but were seldom referred to as the easy virtue gals they really were. If the good girls were pale pastel, these ladies were vivid red. Tough talking and hard drinking, at least their presence and activities had some basis in fact.

But the ultimate victim of the Hollywood Western experi-ence was the American Indian. If probable psychotic killers like Jesse James and Billy the Kid were lionised, the Indians reaped the leftover hostilities and took them on the chin – or in the back, as was also usual on the screen of the Thirties. For the next twenty years, until the mould was finally changed if not destroyed with *Broken Arrow* (Hollywood's first acknowl-edgment of Indians as real people), they were constantly portrayed as a sinister lot – blood, whiskey and scalp thirsty.

Unfortunately, the opinions and prejudices that arose out of this constant blackwash have lasted until today. As a flagrant example of what Hollywood and, particularly, director Cecil B. DeMille thought, there's a scene in *Unconquered* where star Gary Cooper is cornered in a tree with his sidekick who'd dropped his powder horn on his way up the branches. Chasing Indians go by underneath them, but the last one spies the horn, stops and rides back to investigate. As Cooper's knife silently plunges into the Indian's chest, and he falls from his horse, the sidekick looks at Cooper and mutters, 'Well there's *one* good Indian!' (Florid director DeMille was never one for subtlety as evidenced by his casting Boris (Frankenstein) Karloff as the Indian chief!)

The Indian was constantly depicted as the aggressor, spending as much time at his war paint pots as he did killing game for his family. Massacres were a constant theme, but it was only the Indians who were responsible for them, never the whites. One line of dialogue that so-called Indian actors always got was 'White man speak with forked tongue.' At least with that line they got to speak the truth. There *was* a forked tongue, and it belonged to the script writer.

The next major upheaval in the persona of the hero was due to the effects of World War II. The singing cowboys such as Roy Rogers, Gene Autry and others remained highly popular as week-end babysitting fodder, but more virile heroes like Gary Cooper and John Wayne began to pose other questions. The war had exhibited so many horrors to so many millions that almost naturally the Western began to try to answer the age-old question of why men kill each other. The new hero was a cynical and bitter man, and suddenly the smiling days of Tom Mix seemed a long time ago. His aims were the same, but he'd become too much of a realist to try and achieve them by the old ways. The war had destroyed too many illusions, and now he was more prone to instigating the action rather than stalling it till it became inevitable.

The heroes were suddenly, unexpectedly, tired. Gregory Peck, the star of the hot-blooded *Duel in the Sun* (1946) – perhaps the most sweepingly panoramic and ambitious Western ever made (and producer David O. Selznick's Western equivalent to his *Gone With The Wind*) was suddenly the embittered *Gunfighter* (1950), sitting alone in a barroom, fighting off punk kids trying to trade on his reputation as top gun. He was a survivor, sure, but still he looked at it all and wondered why he'd bothered. And of course there was Gary Cooper in *High Noon* (1952), an ageing sheriff who picks up his gun once again to fight off single-handedly a gang of outlaws while the people he's spent his life protecting cower behind closed doors. Where was the assistance of the townspeople? And, more importantly, since he'd done the best job he could, *why* wasn't it there?

The Freudian Westerns of the late Forties and Fifties asked these same questions, punctuating them with bits of philosophy and psychological lingo completely foreign to the Old West. An excellent example of this genre was Raoul Walsh's *Pursued* (1947) with Robert Mitchum as a mentally disturbed cowboy torn by doubts about his status as an adopted child. Another was *The Man From Colorado* (1948) with Glenn Ford, William Holden and Ellen Drew, with Ford essaying the title role of a psychotic judge. Another, *The Fastest Gun Alive* (1956) shows Ford as a shopkeeper haunted by memories of failing to revenge the killing of his lawman father. He takes on deranged outlaw Broderick Crawford to decide which has the right to the film's title.

For a while these pictures enjoyed a certain distinct popularity and were actually closer to the truth of the Western myth than many of the sugar-coated versions of the Thirties. *Shane* (1953) covered both sides of the ideological road in its parallel stories of the social conflict between hard-working farmers and giant landowners and the more memorable one between Alan Ladd and Jack Palance. A great film directed by George Stevens, *Shane* is one of the best Westerns ever made, full of suspense and gritty action as buckskinned Ladd, a knight errant of the rolling landscape, confronts black-clad hired-gun Palance. Jean Arthur, herself a veteran of several Westerns, most notably DeMille's sprawling *The Plainsman* with Gary Cooper in 1936, plays the lady in the middle, who for a while thinks Ladd might stick around. He doesn't though, in the best tradition of the hero who came, saw, conquered and left again, leaving Arthur and son Brandon DeWilde watching sadly as he goes – 'Will ya ever come back Shane?' asks the youngster. Probably not, we thought, as we watched him amble away into the sunset, taking with him the last vestige of the classic screen hero – the righter of wrongs with no price tag attached.

The new or Dirty Western, as critic Richard Schickel calls them, was presaged by John Sturges' *The Magnificent Seven* in 1960. The story is a simple one: seven gunmen are hired by a Mexican town to protect it from a group of bandits led by Eli Wallach. What's most interesting though is not *what* the seven are doing, but *why*. Some are in it because they're broke and need money, one because he's fleeing the law, another to prove himself a man and a gunfighter – and so it goes. The cast included Yul Brynner, Steve McQueen, Charles Bronson, Robert Vaughn, James Coburn and Horst Bucholz. They are all heroes at the film's end, but essentially they're not much different from the men they've signed on to kill. (It's interesting to note that all the stars of *Seven* went on to star images based in part on the loner reputations they gained from this film, except possibly Vaughn who became a TV star as an adventure hero in *The Man from U.N.C.L.E.*)

Moral ambiguity was in full swing, and while it initially shocked audiences who'd come seeking still another un-ambiguous version of the West they'd grown up with, they were intrigued enough to want more. *The Magnificent Seven* was a precursor of all that followed, coming as it did at the beginning of the Sixties. One thing was certain; the anti-hero was here, and his coming stripped the Western film of much of the false glamour it had been afflicted with in the past.

If a man was shot in the guts, there was blood aplenty to prove it. If he died, he no longer crumpled gracefully to a studio floor but writhed in a vivid display of authentic anguish. The true violence, the *authentic* spirit of the West emerged again as it had so briefly with William S. Hart. Only now it was magnified, distorted and advanced not only by technology but by the exposed darknesses of the human spirit that had been hidden so long under a patina of cleanliness and virtue.

The stage was set for a personification of this new breed of hero, and Clint Eastwood personified him in *Fistful of Dollars*. His alienation was complete, his cool frozen in place; a drifter through the past, caught for a while on a piece of film. Always alone, questions about his allegiance soon answered by the constant evidence that he has only one: himself. The world he is a part of is a hostile place filled with dangers he's spent his life defending himself against. He can trust no one, and *wants* no one to trust him. The audience presumably draws the conclusion that the pressures and terrors of his world aren't so very different from those we face in ours. Eastwood is unlike any hero we've ever seen before, consorting as he does with the lowlife, always on the lookout for a fast buck or a faster woman: he's a totally amoral man. He's an existentialist hero living in a time that demands survival, and that's the only thing he's good at.

A Fistful of Dollars came at a time in our society when morals and mores, both sexual and social, were at the height of the Sixties revolution – a battlefield as littered with victims as any ever fought with real guns and ammunition. The siren song was Timothy Leary's tune in, turn on, drop out and millions of American youths had heard it and were singing it loud and clear. Its effects were evidencing themselves in taste changes in everything from the sublime to the ridiculous. Skirts and boots were going up and hair was going down and in the general hysteria Eastwood appeared as a hard-rock figure to hang some fantasies on – fantasies of every splinter group of society, for he appealed to them all.

Blacks immediately loved him because he didn't take any crap from anybody and instead of raising his voice about it, he raised his fist – usually with a gun in it. On New York's 42nd Street, a typical Eastwood movie crowd is like a giant, pulsating, *alive* thing that makes the theatre reverberate with the shouts, yells and roars of approval his mostly black audience lavishes on him.

The young saw him another way, investing *Fistful of Dollars* and its two follow-ups, *For A Few Dollars More* and *The Good, The Bad and The Ugly*, with qualities that combined the best aspects of a good tab of acid and a pile of terrific comic books. He enabled them to have an orgy of inner vision, heightened by their LSD-coloured glasses. It was both funny and frightening as, at other times, his extreme sense of isolation pierced the private loneliness of their own minds.

He was also an instant hit with Middle America, and its hard-hat mentality, who found in him a substitute safety valve for their own growing impatience with a world that seemed to be betraying them. Race riots, student revolutions and drug-scare headlines were alienating them from the society they had to take responsibility for creating, or at least upholding. In many cases even their family unit seemed suddenly too complex for understanding. The same people who'd egged John Wayne on over the years, now saw in Clint a renewed, fresh strength of the kind a tiring Wayne had to put by as increasing age slowed his much imitated step. (Also, Wayne's brush with cancer in the early Sixties had undermined his image, even though, like a true good guy, he'd conquered it.)

The manly view that Hays removed from Westerns in the Thirties, that call of the wild, has always had a healthy ingredient of sexuality in it for it depicts a time and a place where strict morality is unknown and a man takes what he wants any way he can. That sexually aggressive message is what Eastwood is also telegraphing since it's an integral part of his appeal. It's written all over him from the moment he comes on camera, especially in the *Dollar* movies, as he first stalks into town. Everybody reacts – the women are titillated while the men, sensing his innate competitiveness, reach for their guns, that Western symbol of manhood, ready to use it to vanquish the intruder – only to find they can seldom get it up fast enough.

Women have many opinions of Clint Eastwood. Few hold middle ground – they either can't get enough of him, pretend total immunity to him, or hate his pictures and all they stand for. His treatment of women isn't of much current value to any liberated ladies. He's the classic Strong Silent Type that women have only been half joking about meeting for years. For those that like him, he's the most outrageous fantasy figure to some along since a young Gable, Cooper, or Errol Flynn last kept them up on the Late Show. He differs from them because he's a product of *today*. Women in his movies are treated with about as much emotion as he uses in cleaning his gun, which is quickly, efficiently, kept in well-oiled working order and then put aside until he needs it again. He's a throw back who gives even the most militant of ladies a harmless crack at the kind of fantasies mom had during *Gone With The Wind*. She may well park the car, buy the tickets, get the popcorn and choose the seats, but she's also probably picked the movie in the first place! Eastwood is a 6 ft. 4 in. question mark who says more by his silence than any number of other stars do with pages of dialogue. In fact many women prefer him *not* to talk, but rather to act and let them fill in the whys and wherefores. Besides, the promise they see in his green eyes couldn't be put in simple words anyway!

He was known as The Man With No Name in the 'Spaghetti Westerns' and that's the label that's stuck most tightly to his muscular frame. It's a constant nobody seems to be tiring of.

The term Spaghetti Western is as generic to the Sixties as are the Beatles, Andy Warhol, LSD and the whole spectrum of things that fall under the general heading of Pop Culture, yet its history is almost as old as our own. Westerns have been made in many European countries since just after the turn of the century. French filmmakers were first enamoured of this breed of film about the time Porter was making *The Great Train Robbery* over here. There were shoot-em-up one-reelers with titles like *Hooligans of the West* and *The Hanging at Jefferson City*, but they reflected the intense interest Europeans have always felt about our country and its settlement. Even in those days, when we were not the strongest nation in the world, and therefore not a trend setter, the settling of our country was a theme that intrigued them endlessly. Besides the French, the English made Westerns, as well as the Germans – themselves innovators in the use of film and the discovery of much of its basic technology. Germany in particular was interested in depicting our West as seen through the eyes of Americans, with a particular predilection towards the works of James Fenimore Cooper. In the Twenties they turned out many of his classics, including a version of *The Last of the Mohicans* which starred Bela Lugosi. During the Thirties and Forties they continued making Westerns, most notably a long and successful series that starred Hans Albers, one of their first great movie idols.

Since then our legends have been movie material for almost every other country as well – Mexico, Japan, Russia, India, Sweden, Brazil and South Africa to name just a few. They gradually evolved differently under different banners. The Germans, for instance, make film after film based on their own Zane Grey, a writer named Karl May who gave them a host of clichéd characters named Old Shatterhand, Old Surehand and the noble Indian Winnetou, among others.

In the early Sixties it was actually the Germans who resuscitated the European-made Western with these noble tales, quickly dubbed Sauerkraut Westerns – which were popular enough all over the world to breathe new life into the careers of such on-the-skids actors as Stewart Granger and Lex Barker. At one point both men were Germany's top stars, but their reputations never made it in America. The few Sauerkraut Westerns that did cross the ocean went almost directly into second-run houses and drive-ins.

But it was the Italians who soon took over, investing their films with such an amoral, surrealistic intensity that they instantly caught fire everywhere, especially in America. *Fistful of Dollars* was the one that opened the door to a new industry whose basic formula was to grab a 'name' actor, or one they could make into a name, cast him in a darkly squalid setting, and, literally, turn him loose. The action of *Fistful, For a Few Dollars More* and *The Good, The Bad and The Ugly*, Eastwood's three contributions to the new industry, plus that of the dozens of sequels and take-offs is invariably set just south of or around the American border down Mexico way. The setting explains the constant swarthiness of the Mediterranean-looking cast. The desert is always the setting and the time is our Civil War period or just after it. The most common hero of these films is the lone gunman, the stranger, who instigates the action simply by riding into town.

Director Sergio Leone is called the father of the Spaghetti Western, and it's been a continuing source of fame for him. Besides the *Dollars* films, as Eastwood's three are known, Leone has made *Duck You Sucker* with Rod Steiger and James Coburn – already well-established stars when they entered the macaroni sweepstakes – and the highly respected *Once Upon a Time in the West* which starred Henry Fonda, Charles Bronson, Claudia Cardinale (in a rare star female part for Leone), and Jason Robards. And if he's the father of the genre, then he's also the father of the particular anti-hero that has made Clint Eastwood a star.

Intellectual film magazines have sermonised endlessly in the undercurrents of religion, social comment and underlying morality of these films, but their appeal has hardly been a spiritual one. Religion itself is non-existent in them; instead, Leone depicts a brutal world of magic and horror. It is an essentially womanless world, where females are constantly ill used, handled indifferently, or simply not in evidence – they certainly are not an integral or important part of the plot. His style and emphasis have been compared to American directors like Howard Hawks and William Wellman, among others, yet it remains singularly his own. His good guy is consciously aware of the kind of world in which he finds himself. He is amused by it – something Eastwood is especially good at – and chooses to remain aloof from it, knowing that no matter how much evil he might eliminate, the world will quickly spawn more. He's interested in money but doesn't have a definite purpose for it once it's his. His main concern seems to be 'let me alone to live my life in my own style', showing others that he knows how to live, how to face danger with a cool amusement, without fear, and if absolutely necessary, how to die. (In one scene in *Fistful*, Eastwood is supposedly ambushed by the villainous Ramon but emerges from the carnage – through a screen of smoke no less – unscathed, a mystic survivor, and therefore according to some, a new Christ offering a way to face life!)

Leone's bad guys combine all the visual nastiness our own American pictures depicted in the Thirties plus a contemporary sense of bloodthirstiness that makes them instantly revolting. Although neither hero nor villain is morally defined, it's obvious by comparison which is which – but you do need to search for the differences. If sex is an emotionless act for the good guy, it's purely clinical for the bad guy – an act of corruption rather than love, best depicted Leone-style in *Once Upon a Time in the West* when villain Henry Fonda sadistically seduces Claudia Cardinale in an act which quickly turns into rape.

The good guy and the bad guy in Leone's private world have a grudging respect for each other to the point of recognising the similarities in their style, but they also recognise early on that destiny demands they eventually shoot it out. Oddly enough, Leone's villains are a livelier bunch than his heroes, especially Eastwood. In *The Good, The Bad and The Ugly*, Eli Wallach's lusty bandit is a man audiences enjoy as he goes inexorably along his evil way. It's almost as if the baroque vastness of Leone's canvas can support them all until the showdown comes, and then at least two must find themselves at deadly odds. On such a canvas, almost anything is acceptable. A haphazard world of malcontents and rebels, whores and hangmen, and every kind of hero – there is no firm guideline for survival other than the one that works.

As an actor, Clint Eastwood suited his new role in a manner too natural to have been acquired. There's little about him that fits the mould of movie star – including the way he got there. George Hamilton loves to tell that he feels he was the last product of the MGM star stable. 'More stars than there are in heaven' read the ads when they launched him in the late 1950s. He may well be just that. But he is also an example of what went wrong with the machinery in its dying days. Clint was rejected by that same star-making machine at Universal Studios. Yet, as time has proven, his worn cowboy boots have become more potent with movie goers than Hamilton's patent-leather loafers.

While not a product of studio propaganda – carefully groomed and carefully shepherded from one place to another all nicely choreographed for fan magazine lay-outs and autographed eight-by-tens – Eastwood has made it to the uppermost ranks of stardom. In many ways he's as much a loner and drifter offscreen as he is on, but that's because he chooses to be. Send your dollar and a half away for a picture of Clint Eastwood and you'll likely get it, but without the standard capped-teeth 'good luck and best wishes' bit – that's just not his style.

The Early Years

California has always occupied a special niche in the consciousness of America. It's the land of milk and honey, the last outpost of a vast and turbulent society, and has for generations been looked on by thousands of restless citizens as an earthbound slice of that pie in the sky – a land of sunshine and golden dreams. It's homegrown industry, the movies, has largely perpetuated this myth (everybody knows *The Grapes of Wrath* was a communist-inspired fallacy conceived to sidetrack the American Dream!) and yearly, dissatisfied people from all over make their pilgrimages to the sun-washed shores of the Pacific, only to be confronted by the reality of a land that's hardly ever been real to begin with. If Hollywood is a state of mind, then California is a state of dreams where sooner or later everyone wakes up.

Clint and Ruth Eastwood knew a lot about California, and they learned it all the hard way – the same way their only son was to learn it in the three years after his birth in San Francisco on May 31st, 1930. Clint's father was trained as a cost accountant, but in the Great Depression that then lay like a pall over the nation, accounting jobs were non-existent. Clinton senior worked at whatever he could find wherever he could find it. He usually pumped gas for short stints that took the young family from town to town, traversing the northern parts of California from Bakersfield to Marysville, from Redding to Eureka. They stayed until the job ran out and it was time to move on.

Clint was nicknamed Sonny or Junior, both of which he instantly hated, feeling that 'a kid deserves his own name', and in those bleak years it was just about the only thing anybody did have. There was no chance of making any lasting friendships as the Eastwoods made their way from one short-lived job to another. This early isolation no doubt helped form the

28

pattern of strict individuality that has dominated Eastwood's life ever since. 'It was during the Depression, and for my father jobs were hard to come by and hard to maintain. I must have gone to ten different schools in ten years.' His sister Jeanne was born a few years later, and she joined the family's odyssey from one frame house to another in the series of long forgotten towns in which she and her older brother were to grow up. Clinton senior, an educated man caught up short like thousands of others in the Great American Dropoff of the Thirties, displayed a gutsy strength about life that he passed on to his children. He cautioned his son that life was a struggle that required battle-line readiness, instilling in him from an early age a private system of checks and balances that eventually led Clint junior to the decision that there was only one person in his life he could truly count on – himself.

'My father always kept telling me you don't get anything for nothing, and although I rebelled, I never rebelled against that.' Clint's rebellion was a more personal one, one that was etched into his personality during these young years of constant up-rooting, and as he grew, often the tallest member in the new classes he joined for a semester or two, it became a nagging part of him that only time would cure. And that time would come when he was old enough to find out about life on his own. How many nights must he have asked himself if life were meant to be the struggle that it had been and was for him and his family? And how many other nights must he have listened to the train whistles, wishing he was on one, headed away from what he already knew and into something new and different.

He admired his father's strength in keeping his family together, but the long hours it required left little time for the man to get to know his lanky, quiet son. As the years went by, the gulf widened and the only way out was a still long-distant maturity. 'I was never an extrovert but I longed for inde-pendence,' he said once to an interviewer, hastening to add, 'even though I got along great with my parents.' Studio-processed biographies of Eastwood have been vague about the early part of his life, and yet it's obviously been significant to his later development as a loner. It accounts for the remote shyness that remains today an unchanged part of his personality, both onscreen and off. The loneliness of these years persists in his pursuit of privacy even now that he's a star.

His mother Ruth attempted to bring to each temporary home a sense of warmth and family unity, but often the simple realities of day-to-day struggle tangled the thread of stability she tried so hard to weave through her family's life. Clint's grandmother had a small chicken ranch near Sunol, California, and until his family finally settled in Oakland, across the bay from San Francisco, it was the closest thing to a permanent home he knew as a youth. His early years were dotted with visits to it, and for him and his sister it must have seemed an oasis of stability amid the packing and unpacking that was so much a part of their lives.

Clint was a teenager when his father finally got a good job with the Container Corporation of America and moved his family to Oakland, California where at last they were able to put down some roots. Oakland was new territory, a fresh start, and Eastwood prepared to deal with it on the only terms he knew. Whether it was the scantiness of his education or the fact that working with his hands was what he was most comfortable with, Clint enrolled at Oakland Technical High School, and made an attempt to join in the school activities, even though being just one of the guys was something alien to him. He'd reached his full height of 6 ft. 4 in. by those days and the most obvious way for him to make friends was to capitalise on his height by trying out for the school basketball team. Accustomed to a regular routine of physical workouts – he'd had part-time jobs in his youth as often as he could find them – he joined in the team spirit and practised hard, trying to make up for the many years he'd spent on nobody's team but his own.

Even then, Clint had the ability to get what he wanted through sheer determination. Before he finished high school, he was one of the mainstays of the school team and even, for a brief time, considered making basketball a career. His talent on the court was good, but it's doubtful that it was the stuff professionals are made of. Yet in those adolescent years, it must have seemed a normal dream, a reachable goal.

His talent on the court plus his lean good looks and low, deceptively gentle voice made him a favourite with the girls, too, but he never seriously considered getting involved with any particular one. No doubt he remembered the fate of his own parents who'd married young and full of enthusiasm only to have the dream wear away to a workworn veneer of chipped aspirations and scarred struggle. A solitary youth, he concentrated on what he thought he'd need, studying the courses he felt would best equip him for his future, working with his hands rather than just his brain. After all, his father was an educated man and how far had that got him? If Clint ever had to work in a garage, he wanted to do more than pump gas.

Though just what he wanted to do with his life was still a mystery over and above the chancy idea of going into pro basketball, Clint knew what he didn't want to do, and that was to act! His high school English teacher decided that she wanted him to star in the class play. She approached him with the idea one day after class only to be firmly put down. Clint wasn't about to expose himself before his hard-won friends and classmates in an area where he was so unsure of himself, and he let her know it. He later admitted that his first reply to her wasn't a very gentlemanly one and explained, 'I wanted to go out for athletics. Doing plays was not considered the thing to do at that stage of life – especially not presenting them before the entire senior high school.' It had taken Clint too long to establish himself in the school community, and he wasn't about to jeopardise that by making a fool of himself in a play!

Another reason for his refusal apparently was that Eastwood didn't want to be chosen to do something just because of his good looks. He had found them a handicap. People tend to be put off by truly good looks, even in California where there are more good-looking people than most places. In 1946, at Oakland Tech, good looks were something Clint would just as well have liked to forget. In his private world, it wasn't how you looked that mattered, but what you did – and how well you did it.

The title of that play has been long forgotten by Eastwood, but eventually he was persuaded to take part in it when he

learned that some of his other classmates would share the unwanted limelight with him, even though that didn't in any way
insure the production's success. In fact, 'it was really dis-
astrous. We muffed a lot of lines. I swore that was the end of
my acting career.' He found out acting was harder than it
looked during those Saturday matinées he'd gone to with his
younger sister. 'I'd seen a million movies, but up to that point
the closest I'd got to acting was making a pistol out of my
hand, hunkering down behind the seat in front of me, and
shooting back at the screen.'

Despite the unaccustomed solvency of his family's new life,
Clint still hankered after the independence he'd been brought
up to respect. Between semesters he continued taking part-time
jobs, getting used to dealing with adults in their world. Clint
has always had the ability to listen when a subject he doesn't
know about comes up, and during this period he had many
chances to do just that, filing away for future use the information he picked up. (A habit he's continued over the years
and which proved invaluable to him during the short time he
was under contract at Universal. While waiting for his brief
entrances and quicker exits, he stored away the everyday facts
about moviemaking, all of which he utilised years later when he
came to direct his first film, *Play Misty For Me*.)

There were Northern California-type jobs he took when he
had the free time, like hay baling in Yreka, and several stints
with the Forest Service. He liked the woods, the calmness, the
space of it all, and the time he spent as a fire fighter up near
Paradise, California, introduced him to a way of life he liked
enough to pursue when he left high school.

Clint graduated from Oakland Tech in 1948, and felt that
now his education – or as much of it as he then wanted – was
all neatly tied up and finished, and it was time to get out on his
own. His personal need for privacy wasn't the kind that four
walls could provide, and nearby San Francisco put further
impositions on it. Clint wanted out, to find it on his own terms.
Eastwood's formula for privacy is a complex one, but its cornerstone is caution. He moves cautiously, speaks cautiously or
not at all, (a trait that film reviewers have been taking him to

task for, especially since he's been producing his own films) and he acts cautiously. In the world in which he grew up, a man not in total control of himself, his reflexes and emotions, was a man who laid himself open to mistakes, and that kind of man is a fool in Eastwood's vernacular. Like The Man With No Name character, he zealously works to keep his vices, whatever they are, out of sight so as not to incite another man's aggression by the knowledge of his weaknesses. Eastwood doesn't smoke, never has, drinks very little, and when he does, it's Olympia beer.

When he left his Oakland home in the summer of '48, with his high school diploma carefully stashed away in his suitcase, Clint had no definite plan in mind. For the first time in his life there were no appointments to keep, nobody to check in with, and no part-time job to go to the minute school was out. America, just three years out of World War II, was slowly emerging into a peacetime economy but there was plenty of room for a young man who wanted to work and drink a few careful beers while he did so. He headed north through the familiar country of his childhood, seeing again the numerous towns and truck stops he'd once been stuck in, only now he was finally able to keep right on going.

Ending up in Springfield, Oregon, just outside of Eugene, Clint went to work for the Weyerhauser Lumber Company, using his summer jobs as references and his rangy, hard-muscled frame as proof he was as capable of lumberjacking as anybody on the company's crew. 'We were really out in the woods,' he recalled later, 'I was just a kid, but I was strong and could chop down trees with the hard men in that country. The pay seemed pretty good at the time – I earned $1.80 an hour. The wages were high because the work was seasonal. In the cold months the camp closed down. I lived in a camp with the other loggers, and we worked from sunup to sundown. It was a rugged life, and at the end of the day we were too tired to do anything but fall into our bunks.' A regimented, totally masculine environment was his first proving ground, and he drifted into its routine as easily as he had any other, picking up the habits of the other men, learning the language of the woods, and generally being one of the guys.

'Saturday nights were different. We'd go into town and get drunk. I thought those movies about rough-and-ready lumberjacks were exaggerated. Maybe they were, but not much. One night I was standing at the bar of a saloon in Springfield when another logger punched me in the face without warning. Before you knew it, the whole place was in the damnedest fight I ever saw.'

When the cold season started and snow began to gather in the Oregon Hills, Clint and the other loggers broke camp, but Eastwood wasn't ready yet to move on and went to work in the company's pulp mill, living alone in a small cabin. It was rough, but it appealed to him, as if five and a half months around people were enough for a while and he needed a private respite to think things over. The mill job was hard and dangerous, but the challenge intrigued him, as it had when he pitted himself against experienced lumbermen.

'Around Eugene, in the Willamette Valley, it's beautiful, but in the winter it really socks in. You go six, seven months without seeing blue.' When Clint had enough of it, he left, heading towards Seattle. His family had recently moved to, Seattle because Clint senior had a better job. Clint just showed up there one day and eased back into the family circle as simply as he'd left it, but he didn't make any long range plans to remain. 'It was good to get back to civilisation for a while, but I missed the woods.'

While he lived in Seattle, Clint took whatever jobs turned up, including a short stint pumping gas. Next he took a job at the Bethlehem Steel plant, stoking the giant furnaces late at night, long after everyone else had gone home. Years later he could quickly recall that job as one of the most unforgettable experiences of his life. It took him away from the outdoors and into a man-made hell where he spent hundreds of hours repeating the same actions over and over, feeding the hungry bellies of the plant. 'My job was general maintenance around the big blast furnaces, and the heat got so intense you felt as if your skin would peel right off your body. I didn't like inside work, even though the pay was good. I was working the graveyard shift from midnight until nine in the morning. I had my days

34

free but I was too tired to enjoy them.' He didn't stay there any longer than he had to, and after saving a few bucks, started looking for an easier job, or at least one that would get him back outside.

In the little town of Renton, just outside Seattle, Clint found work as a lifeguard on a public beach in King County. 'It paid hardly anything, but there I was sitting out in the sun, checking out all the pretty little chicks in their bathing suits. The fringe benefits were great. Believe me, those jobs were hard to get.'

At that age there wasn't any particular ambition that kept him on the move. Just the sheer fact of doing it seemed reward enough. He always did his job, took his pay, and either came back for another week or split for something else. After the beach scene faded, Clint went to work in the parts department of the Boeing Aircraft plant in Renton. 'People would call for parts, and you'd get them stuff out of the inventory, fill out the forms, and ship it. And I drove a truck, short trip stuff, and loaded and unloaded siding for the Color Shake organisation in Seattle.'

He soon realised the home siding business wasn't the challenge he was looking for either. As he gradually neared twenty-one, the age when in society's eyes the boy becomes a man and either begins to assume the responsibilities of one or gets classified as a bum, Eastwood's own background began to assert itself and he realised his life needed some kind of purpose, a definite goal.

Since his early youth, Clint had purposely surrounded himself with every type of man from the rough-and-ready loggers to the drifters he'd shared coffee with in a hundred roadside diners. He'd had ample chance to study the ones who'd taken life as it had been dealt them and the ones who'd chosen a definite route. He'd observed the fate of those who'd never grabbed hold of an ambition and had slipped slowly from easy-going young manhood into an adulthood that became bitter as the years went by. The results of his tally scared him, but it also made him think. The lure of the highway suddenly seemed less fascinating when he realised he wasn't going anywhere special on it – there were plenty of stops along the way but no real destination.

Though it sounds incongruous now, it was about this time that Clint began thinking of going to college. He thought he'd like to major in music. He didn't have any special talent in the field, but it interested him. Later in his acting career he actually did take a stab at making records, plus starring in the musical *Paint Your Wagon*. But he's never been accused of overlooking a great musical talent.

These thoughts were germinating in his head as he made his way back over and through the small towns of the Northwest. The decision as to what he was to do, however, was made for him. In an infrequent call to his family in Seattle, he learned he'd received a message that starts, 'Greetings from the President of the United States.' Clint Eastwood was in the Army!

The Army and
Maggie Johnson

Many a grizzled veteran has testified over the years that the Armed Forces have been the salvation of thousands of wandering youths and eventually, though mostly through luck, this was what it turned out to be for Clint Eastwood. The Army gave him a foothold towards the mainstream of society and a chance to expand his future with his natural resilience tempered by responsibility and orderliness. One of his great gifts has always been to accept the unavoidable when it was obvious there was little he could do to alter it. He went into the service in this frame of mind, confident it would eventually prove worth his time.

He reported to Fort Ord, California for basic training and slipped into the rigorous routine as though he'd been practising for it all his life. He'd always had a soldier's mentality whether he knew it or not, plus the lone-wolf streak that one needs to put a job ahead of any other considerations. There were no love letters from back home arriving to unsettle him, and he didn't look for a local interest – the thought never occurred to him. His work-hardened body met the demands of the sixteen weeks of basic training with energy to spare, and his mind clicked quickly into the pattern of service life conformity. He brought with him the ways of the road, the easy-going good-naturedness and acceptance that life had taught him plus the streak of curiosity that had already made his head a stockpile of information on which he could draw when circumstances demanded. The lone wolf joined the pack pretty much on his own terms, and while he never won any battles except the one inside himself, he was to leave the service after his two-year stretch a wiser man.

One of the old saws about the Army is that it seldom gives a man a job to do in which he's had any previous experience. Clint was luckier than a lot of his fellow recruits. His expertise as a swimmer brought him to the attention of his superiors, and he started out as a lifeguard/instructor to the dry-footed recruits and ended up running the entire operation. 'I love swimming. I had the pool to myself except when they gave swimming classes to recruits. Of every twelve guys who took the swimming test, ten sank immediately. My job was to pull them out.'

Clint considered himself very lucky that he never got shipped overseas to active duty. He admits he wasn't above using a little of his con-artist talent to make sure of it. He volunteered to help out at the pool regularly, selling himself to his commanding officer by saying, 'I was absolutely the greatest swimmer going, things like that, and I ended up getting the job. When we started out, there was this buddy of mine and me, a master sergeant and four sergeants over us, and a lieutenant over them. Everybody got shipped to Korea except me; my name just never came up. So I figured I'd make the best of it and went up and talked to the captain. I said, "Look, I'm only a private, but I think I can handle the swimming pool thing," and he said, "Well I don't even know how to swim, so go ahead and run it. You're wearing a sweat shirt; nobody will know you're just a private." So I stayed there and hired four other guys to work for me. We had a pretty good swimming instruction programme going, got quite a few excellent ratings – like four-star movie reviews. I even lived down at the pool; it was a terrific deal for being in the service.'

A very good deal indeed! So good and so easy, in fact, that Clint was able to do a little private hustling on the side, taking some jobs off the base to build up a cash reserve he spent on having a good time. He was so used to hard work that the easiness of his Army job left him feeling guilty – he hadn't yet learned that if you're lucky enough to do what you like and get paid for it, too, then you're way ahead of the game. He knows that now.

While the other guys laid around on their bunks playing cards, sleeping and generally wasting their free time, Clint took a job with the Spreckles Sugar Refinery near the base. He worked in the plant's warehouse, hefting fifty-pound sacks of sugar and stacking them for shipment. 'It was hard work,' he admits, 'but they paid me $1.70 an hour.' He found it hard to live on the meagre $76 a month the Army paid him. During his frequent off-base manoeuvres, he'd 'run through that in a couple of nights with the girls. I *had* to have more money.'

Money to Eastwood has always meant the ability to move around, to do things his way. Even now that he's a multi-millionaire and one of the most powerful men in the movie industry, you'd never know it from what he spends. His family is exceedingly comfortable but not lavishly kept, and his personal lifestyle remains close to what it's always been. In a land of technicolor dreams, his personal life is black and white in comparison to many other stars. Money is power, the power to call the shots, and that's always been more important to him than a fancy wardrobe or a Rolls Royce. Status symbols are so foreign to his self-image that a graffiti artist in a New York subway summed it up beautifully when he wrote, 'Clint Eastwood wears Gucci shoes.' That's just not his style.

The stratified society of Army life enabled him to study carefully the men in power. After quitting the sugar plant, he was hired to tend bar in the Non-commissioned Officers' Club – the hangout of the men who'd won their ranks and stripes the hard way. Frequented by veterans of past wars and up-and-coming youngsters like himself, all had a story to tell and usually Clint found there was a lesson for him in it somewhere. Located just off the base, the club was a place where the men let their medals slip a little as they unwound, and Clint listened and observed, judging what it was that made them tick.

It didn't pay as well as the sugar job, but there were other compensations. Besides, 'It was easier work and I could drink a half dozen beers a night on the job.'

Eastwood was in the service for only two years. They were hectic years, and for the first time since high school he had an opportunity to relate to men his own age. Not that he had many friends, because Clint never had a great need for inti-mate friends, he just needed somebody from time to time to

39

swap a few tales with over a beer. One friend – a dentist who was dating a girl from the University of California at Berkeley – suggested that he and Eastwood spend a week-end at Berkeley. His girl had a friend they thought would get along well with Clint. Clint had his own engagements for the week-end, two of them in fact, but he went along with his buddy. The girl he met that week-end was Maggie Johnson, a pert blonde coed at Berkeley, and they did hit it off.

'I met Maggie at the sorority house. It was no such thing as love at first sight but we liked one another right away.' Their first evening together was a far cry from the dates he was used to on his few free nights. In fact they didn't do much more than just sit in a bar, 'had a few brews' as he calls it, and talked. It was the start of a good relationship – very different from any previous relationship with a woman that he had been involved in. He'd found a woman he could talk to, who would listen to him and, most important, who wasn't afraid to talk back!

It was the first of many dates they were to have – whenever Clint could make it up from Fort Ord and Maggie wasn't busy. There weren't any commitments, just having fun doing all the things everybody else was doing in the early Fifties: going to movies, dancing, eating lots of inexpensive Italian food, and getting to know more about each other. She wasn't the only girl he dated, and she didn't wait around the sorority house for him to call either.

When he could swing it, Clint would take a week-end pass and fly to Seattle to see his family. Now no longer a part of their everyday life, Clint and his parents and sister Jeanne were closer than they'd ever been when living under the same roof. He liked visiting his home, possibly because he knew it would only be for a short while – and they seemed to enjoy his visits as well. Once he hitched a ride back to Monterey on a small service plane, but he almost didn't live to tell the tale. It crashed into the Pacific off Point Reyes, and Clint was thrown clear but without a life-jacket. The pilot was wearing the only one. He swam three miles in pitch black ocean before he got ashore. 'We both made it, but I had the most work to do. I didn't mind the swim, but that five-mile hike before I found a highway really bothered me.' When Clint told Maggie what happened, he just laughed it off as nothing much out of the ordinary.

Maggie Johnson Eastwood is one of Hollywood's mystery women. She seldom takes part in any of the usual publicity activities that take up the time of so many other movie stars' wives. Usually her only appearances are beside her husband at a major charity premiere or the Academy Awards. As the wife of one of Hollywood's most prominent stars, she would, of course, be welcome wherever she might choose to go, but Maggie prefers the kind of life her husband does – a private one. It's no secret that their marriage is a real partnership and that when she has something to express, either personal or professional, Clint listens to her and often heeds her advice. He listens because he trusts her.

After she graduated from Berkeley, Maggie moved to Los Angeles. She landed a job with an L.A.-based exporting company that specialized in auto parts. It wasn't long before Maggie heard from Clint, who was thinking over what he wanted to do now that there wasn't a commanding officer around to give him orders.

There weren't many options open, but just before he left the service a couple of things had happened that had given Clint something new to think about. While stationed at Ford Ord, he met actors David Janssen and Martin Milner. Their service stretches gave him an opportunity to observe them. He overcame his prejudices and misconceptions about actors and decided they were real people – no better, no worse, and more important, no less masculine because of their theatrical careers. He gradually overcame the antagonism he'd felt in high school when he had been tapped for that school play.

Another thing that helped change his mind was Universal Studio's using Fort Ord for location-shooting on a film they were doing, allowing Clint to get a close-up view of movie-making. One day on chow line, the film's assistant director introduced himself to Clint and told him he thought he had what it took to be a movie actor. Then Clint was introduced to the picture's director who was also impressed by the handsome soldier with the lazy grin. The director told him if he was interested in pursuing the subject when he finished his service stretch, to look him up at the studio in Hollywood, and he'd try and arrange a screen test. Clint's reaction was initially sceptical, but he filed the information away, figuring, what the hell, it couldn't hurt to investigate.

Eastwood and a couple of buddies hit Los Angeles in February of 1953, intent on using the G.I. bill to continue their educations. Everybody but Clint, that is. He had an appointment to keep and wanted to check it out before making any other decisions. When he got to Universal, he was told the director he was looking for was no longer working there. He had his G.I. bill, and since it didn't seem as if the acting bit was going to work out, he thought about returning to Seattle and using it at the University of Washington. Then he remembered Maggie Johnson and gave her a call.

They both quickly found that the mutual interest they'd shared during his three-day passes hadn't diminished, and both being new in a strange town, it was good to see a friendly face. During their conversations over the days that followed, Maggie was quick to point out to Clint that acting was the first definite career he'd ever been interested in. She encouraged him to stick around and try to break into the movie world. Also, now that she'd found him again, she didn't want him to go. He decided to give L.A. a try and enrolled at Los Angeles City College, to major, as he said, 'in Business Administration. That's what every student does who hasn't the faintest idea of what he wants to do when he graduates.'

Hollywood may well have been the land of golden daydreams for some in the early Fifties, but to Clint it was just another place to start from scratch. As usual, the money coming in wasn't enough to keep him happy (the G.I. monthly allotment was only $110) so he began scouting out some part-time jobs to supplement his Army money. One of his first jobs was at a Signal Oil gas station on Santa Monica Boulevard that, as he laughed about later, was right across the street from the unemployment office. That job made him a couple of bucks an hour and also had the advantage of being close to the beach where he could go every afternoon for a quick swim. In addition, he made a deal with the owner of the small apartment building where he was living to do the supervising of the place: replacing light bulbs, hauling out the trash, changing fuses and anything else that needed doing in exchange for free rent.

With his classes in the morning, the gas station in the afternoons, and managing the building at night, there wasn't much free time for anything else. Getting serious over a girl – especially since there were so many around, didn't occur to him. He and Maggie saw much of each other, but there was no talk of making it permanent. They both went out with others, but Clint kept coming back to see her. A feeling of easy compatability slowly grew between them – a feeling very different from any he'd ever felt about a woman before. Until Maggie, Clint's relationship with the opposite sex was simple. He needed women sexually, period. Maggie made him realise a woman could be a friend, a lover, a companion and an equal, and that took a lot of getting used to on his part.

The first of his new jobs to go was the apartment superintending – 'I hated listening to all the old ladies complain about flaking paint and leaking water pipes.'

His Army buddies, Janssen and Milner, were getting their acting careers off the ground after their service detours, and Clint kept in floating touch with them. It was tough getting started, they told him, though admitting they had one of the better deals in town. Universal, where they both worked, was one of the few studios at that time giving long-term contracts and grooming their contract people for full-time movie stardom. MGM, once the greatest starbuilder of all, was tapering off their personality machinery in favour of dealing with established stars; and Warner Bros. was about the only other place in town where an unknown could possibly, just possibly, get started.

Clint lost heart for a while. Looking around, he saw that Hollywood was a town filled with good-looking guys and girls from all over the country who'd come there to strike it rich in the movies. Everywhere, working in gas stations, landscape companies and hamburger drive-ins he saw proof of it. He didn't know exactly what the spark was that set one apart from another, but with a lifetime of having been looked at for his own good looks, he knew it wasn't something you found too often. So he stuck it out, hoping he had that special spark.

A still photographer named Irving Lasper encouraged Clint after seeing the results of a few photosessions. By this time Clint had added digging swimming pools to his work load and was frankly getting a little tired of it all. The few months that he'd been in L.A. had been hard ones. Lasper kept urging him on, and when Clint finally agreed to it, helped set up a 'personality' screen test. 'In those days they'd make interview tests, not acting tests. They'd sit you in front of the camera and talk – just talk. I thought I was an absolute clod. It looked pretty good; it was photographed well, but I thought "if that's acting, I'm in trouble!" ' Still, he really was excited about the possibilities.

It wasn't acting, not by a long shot, but there was something about the tall, slow-speaking ex-soldier that struck a chord of interest in the minds of the people whose job it was to screen the taped interviews in hopes of finding a new Clark Gable somewhere among them. When he told Maggie about it, she shared his enthusiasm.

Although they'd been dating others, they still felt most comfortable with each other. It had been an unhurried building of feeling with no rushing into anything on the part of either. Maggie was busy with her job and liked it, although she gradually realised that a business career wasn't what she wanted out of life. During the months they'd been dating in Hollywood, it became more and more obvious to them both that their futures seemed to fit together – that they were good for each other. Maggie knew him, understood him, encouraged him, and the time seemed right for both of them to put down a few roots. Whatever happened, they'd have each other and that looked like a damn good deal.

On December 19th, 1953, months after he'd come to Los Angeles and as the New Year approached, Clint and Maggie got married. It was a happy time and, as usual with Clint, a private one. They had each other, they were young, beautiful;

their whole lives were ahead of them. To add to their happiness, word came from Universal that they liked his test.

Within two months Clint signed a contract with the studio at $75 a week, a sum that looked pretty good after the scrambling of the past year. What pleased him even more was the fact he'd be getting paid for learning how to act – and nobody'd ever paid him something for nothing before.

He and Maggie moved to a small apartment near the studio, and she kept working at her job since his salary was not going to be enough for both of them. Clint was excited. His life suddenly had a direction it had never had before. Though acting was a new endeavour and one in which he had no experience, he recognised it as a new beginning and he was happy. It was the lowest rung on the ladder, in fact he said later 'a little lower than working in the mailroom', but at least the ladder was leaning against something steadier than a gas station wall or a lifeguard's chair.

How Did a Nice Boy like You
Get in a Place like This?

The phrase 'going Hollywood' is one that's pretty much out of use these days, due largely to people like Clint Eastwood. It used to denote a particular kind of American craziness that happened when a studio would take one good-looking gas jockey or former salesgirl, cap their teeth, change their hairline, give them a nose job, photograph them from every angle, and subject them to a publicity blitz that made their new faces visible on every newsstand and in every corner drugstore. Along with the big buildup, you also got such intimate details of their lives as their favourite food, their favourite kind of man or woman, and the real colour of their eyes. (It's a trip, but one that Clint never took.)

When he signed with Universal, it had the only truly viable star-making machine left in Tinseltown. It worked overtime to churn out popular images and memorable names for it's young actors as the first step in grooming them for stardom – which would hopefully be in Universal movies. Very like the old story of the middle-aged man who marries a teenager so he can bring her up the way he wants to. 1954 was the heyday of agent Henry Willson, then known as Hollywood's top name dropper. He'd already come up with Tab and Rock and a few other catchy monikers that seemed to match the tempo of the era. Clint's name was deemed strong enough so he never needed Willson's services in that department. Clint proceeded to join the newly named discoveries in the studio's talent school after a brief stopoff at the publicity department to fill in the blanks of his life before 1954.

He knew a few of the faces when he got there, but there were also plenty of new ones, too, like John Saxon, George Nader and Bret Halsey. The female contingent included people like

46

Lori Nelson, Mara Corday, and the studio's resident blonde bombshell – Mamie Van Doren. The classes covered every subject from which fork to use (in case they were cast in a 'toney' picture, which was any one with more than one fork on the table), to how to (a) for the women, cringe glamorously during jousts and swordfights, and (b) for the men, how to joust and *how* to swordfight! The biggest moneymaker on the lot at that time was Tony Curtis, then peaking as the idol of every bobby-soxer in the country. If the 'Adonis from Gowanus' (as they called him out of earshot in a merciless jibe on his Bronx background), could do it, so could they. That was the rallying cry that echoed loud and clear through the long halls, gymnasiums, riding practice areas and in the classrooms where Curtis was King and Stanislavski was a guy who had a restaurant on Sunset Strip.

The attitude of the studio staffers towards Clint was his first lesson in what it takes to make it out of the novice ranks and into the big money. Clint never liked being told what to do, and when he was advised to stand up straighter and think about having his teeth fixed, he just grinned back, not certain they really meant it. Slumped shoulders or not, though, the studio decided to use him in a sequel to one of the previous year's biggest hits, *The Creature From the Black Lagoon*. The sequel was to be called *The Revenge of the Creature*. Besides the popular Gill Man, it also starred Lori Nelson and John Agar, Shirley Temple's ex-husband. It was to be filmed in 3-D, the camera process that brought the viewer right into the action, like it or not. Clint's character was called Jennings, a lab assistant. To prepare for it he had to practise looking professional in a lab jacket. He appeared in a few scenes, answering short questions with shorter answers and passing around a few beakers. It did get his face up there in a very popular product, even though he was disappointed he didn't have more to do. Talking about it years later, he recalled the futility he felt, a futility so great that he didn't even remember the film's real title – 'My first part was in *The Revenge of the Creature From the Black Lagoon*. I was playing a laboratory assistant walking around with a pair of white mice in my pocket or something. I had about three lines and I can't remember a word of them.'

His next part was in something at least a bit more familiar to him. He played a sailor in *Francis In The Navy*, one of the several Francis the Talking Mule pictures that kept Donald O'Connor in star billing during the Fifties. He filled the sailor togs in reel life as well as he'd ever done Army fatigues in real life, and blended in nicely, contrasting his exceptional face against the comic mugs of O'Connor and Richard Erdman. Martin Milner was in it too, and the two ex-service buddies had a few laughs over the uniform switch.

There wasn't any chance of Clint going Hollywood, even if he wanted to. Five years later as the star of *Rawhide*, he and Maggie chose to live quietly away from the Hollywood social scene, secure in each other. As for those famous Fifties' 'Movie star at home in the kitchen' layouts, there weren't any of those either. Clint's marriage was played down in the little publicity the studio released on him in sharp contrast to what they did when their two top stars, Tony Curtis and Janet Leigh got married. So anxious were they to make sure that every breathless moment of their happiness be recorded, they even took a fan magazine photographer along with them on their honeymoon!

The closest Maggie got to the cameras was during a stint as a bathing suit model for the Catalina swimsuit company. She'd encouraged Clint to take the chance on a movie career and was willing to keep her part of the bargain in whatever way was necessary. It was enough for Clint that he had somebody to talk to when he returned home from a day in front of the cameras. He felt like an expensive piece of merchandise in a Beverly Hills shop. He wasn't crazy about it and swallowed his anger on many occasions, and it wasn't long before he started his personal plan to beat them at their own game. Between those infrequent shots of his, he stood on the sidelines and took mental notes on just how to make a movie. Even then he seemed to know it would someday be useful.

One great advantage of the old studios was that they did give a younger actor as much experience in as many different set-

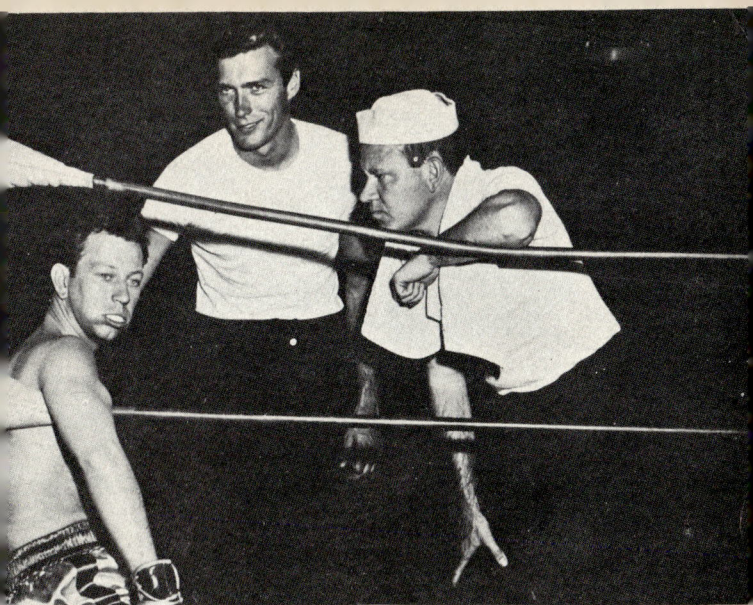

Donald O'Connor, Clint Eastwood and Richard Erdman in *Francis in the Navy*, Clint's second film

The First Travelling Saleslady. David Brian, Frank Wilcox, Dan White, Barry Nelson, Carol Channing, Ginger Rogers (behind bars) and Clint Eastwood

Kim Hunter starred with Eastwood in his first big film, *Rawhide*

Clint as a drifter in *A Fistful of Dollars* with Marriane Koch as Marisol

Eastwood in one of
his grittier roles,
*The Good, The Bad
and The Ugly*

Richard Burton and Clint Eastwood pose as Nazi officers in *Where Eagles Dare*

Clint and Lee Marvin in a scene from the very popular *Paint Your Wagon*

tings as possible. From a lab man to a Navy job, Clint next got a chance to use some of his knowledge of history. The studio cast him as The First Saxon in the Arthur Lubin production *Lady Godiva*. It was a good-natured historical epic whose main asset, especially in technicolor, was its star Maureen O'Hara. Clint's billing in *Francis*, albeit it in fifth place, was good for a newcomer, but in *Godiva* his name was down on the bottom line in the credits. It was another learning experience, though, and gave him a firsthand chance to watch veterans like Oscar-winner Victor McLaglen and Torin Thatcher at work. He gamely joined just about every other young actor on the lot in the tights and chain-mail epic which gave everybody a chance to swing a sword or two around the plaster castle walls. The critics called the picture forgettable, but before Clint could even take off his costume, he'd been set for another bit, this time as a pilot in a monster movie called *Tarantula*.

At least in *Tarantula* he was in for the finish, even if you can't get a good look at him as he sits there in a studio cockpit ordering his fellow pilots to drop the napalm that finally kills the giant spider. An undistinguished quickie, *Tarantula* is a very funny movie that wasn't meant to be so.

After six months Clint's salary was upped to $100 a week, but that didn't persuade him any kind of big break was around the corner, David Janssen was getting a little push from the front offices, and Milner, too, was progressing to bigger roles. Clint was still getting parts with dialogue that could be written on a post card.

It was about this time that Maggie contracted a very serious case of hepatitis and had to quit her job for a year. According to Clint, she got it 'very badly – about as badly as you can get it without ceasing to exist', so he was grateful for the raise even if it wasn't much. It was the first crisis of their marriage, and for a while the outlook was a bleak one with mounting doctor bills plus everyday living expenses. Clint gritted his teeth, went to classes, kept working – and kept watching.

His contract guaranteed him forty weeks of salary a year, so he had plenty of time to watch. He was a familiar figure, towering on the sidelines, waiting to give his all to his one line or so

and then retreat into the shadows to keep an eye on the proceedings. He was getting paid to learn, after all, and to him the
physical business of making the movies was more interesting
than etiquette lessons or fencing practice.

Oddly enough there wasn't anybody on the scene who recognised much more in him than just a handsome face – and in a
backlot crammed with them, that wasn't much of an advantage. He spoke slowly and easily, but there wasn't much
inflection in his voice, almost as if he strove to retain his incon-
spicuous image. As a boy he'd gone with his sister Jeanne to
many Saturday matinee sessions with Gary Cooper and other
stalwart non-actors, and he identified with them rather than
the glib-voiced playboy charmers played by Cary Grant or
Melvyn Douglas.

His exposure and billing in the *Francis* movie had engendered a bit of notice from the critics who called him en-
gaging and, predictably, handsome, but that slim enthusiasm
wasn't reflected where it counted – in the studio mailroom.
While stars like Universal's Tony Curtis, Columbia's John
Derek and 20th's Jeff Hunter racked up thousands of requests
per month for autographed pictures, Clint's mail slot stayed
empty. The studio purposely exposed their players profusely
and in a variety of parts so they'd have a better chance of
recognition in the ticket-buyers' minds. So far, Clint's face was
forgettable.

When his next six-month option was up, and he was eligible
for another $25 per week increase, this fact was brought home
to him forcefully. The front office said they didn't feel he war-
ranted a raise, but that if he agreed to stay at the hundred-
dollar level, they'd pick him up for another half year. 'At first I
was mad, of course, and I said "What the hell, if they can't give
me a raise I'll take a hike." Then I decided I'd better hang in
there another six months and get a little more experience.'

His reward for buckling under was a few more back-to-the-
camera shots and a role in the big budgeted *Never Say Good-
bye* which starred Rock Hudson. It was also to launch a new
European import by the name of *Miss Cornell Borchers*.
(Cornel Wilde was still big in those days, and the studio bosses

weren't taking any chances!) Shot in technicolor, it was ostensibly a vehicle for Hudson, then surpassing Curtis as the studio's top draw. Eastwood's part was again a small one. He shared the screen in only a few scenes with Hudson, but at least it was another credit to his growing list.

Unfortunately it turned out to be his last at Universal. The studio dropped his contract – 'They axed me. I guess I still wasn't worth the $125!' Eighteen months of hard work were finished for him, but he left the studio with a great deal more than when he'd entered it.

When he broke the news to Maggie, she suggested she would try to get some modelling jobs now that she was well enough to work again, and Clint made the rounds to line up an agent for his new career as a free-lance actor. The pickings were slim, and before he knew it he was back behind a pick and shovel, digging swimming pools in Encino.

He thought his luck had finally changed when he signed with RKO Radio Pictures to be in a technicolor comedy called *The First Travelling Saleslady*. Starring were Ginger Rogers, Carol Channing, Barry Nelson and, hopefully, himself. It was directed by Arthur Lubin, another Universal alumnus who'd directed him previously in *Francis in the Navy* and *Lady Godiva*, and it was arranged that he'd have 'introducing' billing in it – a coup for any young actor. As shooting progressed on it, he finally had his first close-up as the love interest of Channing, a tall lady who needed some tall support in this, her first picture. He had a few good scenes and displayed a latent talent for comedy, although the script was far from being a gem of creativity.

He got along well with the stars, and when filming was wrapped up, felt at last he'd made a little positive headway towards a real career. These high hopes were quickly dispelled by the generally poor reviews the picture got – it needed more spice than Ginger could come up with – even with the smattering of 'promisings' he got. However, the studio was pleased with him and cast him in another picture, *Escapade in Japan*, as a screwball pilot nicknamed Dumbo. An East meets West tale of two runaway boys (one former *Lassie* owner Jon Provost), Clint helps them make the getaway that starts them on their adventures across the Japanese countryside.

By the time it was finished, bad luck struck again. Howard Hughes, then the controlling force of the studio, lost interest in moviemaking and sold the studio lock, stock and backlot – including the unreleased movie, which Universal then picked up. They still weren't interested in picking up his contract though, and once again, Clint was out of work.

There were some television spots on action shows like *Navy Log*, *Men of Annapolis* and *Highway Patrol*, but at that time TV was a decided step down after a studio contract. 'TV was like a younger brother, or a second-class citizen. But to me it was a logical place to really learn the business. Most of the people in television were doing the newest things, and in TV you had to work twice as fast, twice as hard to get half the credits. I learned a heck of a lot. I didn't have any giant parts, but they were improvements over what I'd been doing in those B movies – those three or four line bits.'

Clint decided to use some of his muscle-building background and started offering to do any stunt work that might be involved in his part, which saved on the production's payroll. 'Yeah, once in while I'd get a supporting lead because I could ride a motorcycle, jump off a building or some crazy thing.' He still does many of his stunts even now, although big ones, like the motorcycle dive into the San Francisco Bay in *Magnum Force*, he leaves to the pros.

His Universal tenure primarily taught him that there was still a lot he didn't know, and he spent every spare dime on acting lessons, studying at various times with Jerry Becker and Jack Kosslyn in an attempt to get on top of the craft he'd decided he wanted to master. The acting bug had bitten him deeply. Since he and Maggie had decided not to have children for a while, he could afford to experiment a bit and explore all possibilities open to him. 'I decided acting was what I wanted for a career . . . peculiar thing. Most of us feel acting is something you may try for six months or a year as a lark and maybe luck out. But there's no way that'll happen. It takes a long time to establish yourself in the profession.'

It all sounds very good in view of Clint's current success, but those were actually very tough days for Clint and Maggie. One thing that helps immensely to keep them so tightly together has been a sense of humour. Clint's often admitted that what makes Maggie very special to him is that she can make him laugh. Even today, that's not an easy job.

Besides digging swimming pools, Clint interspersed his three-to-four-day acting jobs with occasional detours to the unemployment office. Sometimes months would go by without an acting job.

One friend, George Fargo, recalled his early friendship with Clint and the loyalty that came with it. 'We were working for the United Pool Company and one day I got fired. Anyway the boss looked over and saw Clint unbuttoning his work shirt. "What're *you* doing?" the guy asked Clint. And Clint just said very casually, "George is my friend, he hasn't got a ride home." And he quit just like that.'

One wonders what Maggie thought of this kind of action when it suddenly meant a shorter pay cheque, but it's a quality about Eastwood that stands out with all who know him well. He has a quick temper and doesn't go out of his way to make friends, but once you're in the circle you're in for good unless you do something outrageously offensive to him, such as talking about his loyalty.

More than once during the dry spell he thought about quitting but always reconsidered when Maggie encouraged him to remember some of the good things that had happened and insisted that even greater ones were going to happen if he'd just be patient. 'I couldn't make a full-time living from television, so I dug holes for swimming pools and went back to lifeguarding. When a day's work was done, I'd knock on the doors of agents. But everybody knows agents don't give a damn about young unemployed actors. I even went on unemployment a couple of times while I was trying to find acting jobs, and that began to dishearten me. I couldn't keep bouncing around looking for jobs when my wife was working regularly as a stenographer and as a model in her free time.'

Feeling very discouraged, Clint finally got a chance to make his first Western at 20th Century Fox, a modest oater called *Ambush at Cimarron Pass* – a film he now dismisses as 'one of the worst Westerns ever made'. It starred Scott Brady and was filmed in Regalscope, a colour technique that lasted for a quick year or two in the late Fifties. He played a former Civil War soldier who's out to help settle the West. An undeniable quickie, Clint was way down on the cast list although in its recent Late Show revivals, his name is often listed ahead of Brady's.

William Wellman, the giant director of the Thirties and Forties who made pictures like *A Star Is Born*, *Public Enemy*, and the classic *Battleground*, was preparing a picture at Warner Bros. to highlight the accomplishments and triumphs of the ace World War I flying outfit the *Lafayette Escadrille*, and the call went out for actors, which Clint eagerly answered. He was picked for a small role along with fellow ex-classmates David Janssen and Brett Halsey for the flick which toplined Warner's Great Blonde Hope of the time, Tab Hunter. Bill Wellman, Jr., was in it, too, and the production hoped to trade on both Hunter's popularity and the genius of Wellman, Sr., whose 1929 *Wings* was an established air classic. The picture had plenty of action and scads of publicity, but wasn't the epic Warners had hoped for. It ended up, for Clint anyway, as just another bit part.

Not being billed in the credits except in the 'featured' cast was a letdown to a guy who'd only been 'introduced' two years before. Again Clint began to feel as if his career had been caught in a revolving door that was never going to come unstuck. The anger and frustration of being so continually overlooked was taking its toll on his temper. He seriously thought of chucking the whole venture and returning home to the San Francisco Bay area where he'd spent his teenage years. What was he working so hard for anyway? To spend the rest of his life as a piece of human furniture to be placed somewhere at the whim of some half-baked assistant director? He'd already seen some of his friends hit it big only to disappear with the speed of a fan magazine cover, and his own experiences had taught him that to get even that far required a kind of luck he didn't seem to have.

Clint had made some friends in the industry, and like most actors, visited them when he had the chance. One of them was Sonia Chernus who was employed in the story department of CBS and who was a chum of both Clint and Maggie. One day on the way home from the beach, he stopped by CBS to say hello. He and Sonia headed for the building's coffee wagon to talk and reminisce. While they were chatting, a man walked up to them and interrupted the conversation.

'Are you an actor?' he asked Clint.

'Yeah,' Clint replied.

'What have you done?' the man asked, and by the time Clint was finished spieling off his credits, he'd been asked to join the man in his office when he finished his coffee. Robert Sparks, then CBS Television's executive producer in charge of all the network's programming, was a man who was currently in a bind. The network was preparing a new Western series which they were calling *Rawhide*. The top role of trail boss had already been given to Eric Fleming, but now they were looking for another actor to play his number one ramrod on what has since been called history's longest cattle drive. They needed someone whose personality would contrast favourably with Fleming's, and Sparks was impressed by Eastwood's looks and his easy speech patterns and wanted to talk to him some more.

Once in Spark's office, Clint repeated his credits 'always increasing the importance of the roles by about fifty per cent, praying to God the guy would never ask to see *Ambush at Cimarron Pass*. Which, of course, he did'. The quickness of it all didn't fail to tickle Clint's sense of humour, and the speed with which he found himself selling his talent seemed funnier still. 'I was taking the whole thing kind of lightly because although I knew CBS was casting an hour television show, I'd heard the lead had to be older than me – about thirty-nine or forty. So the man – I didn't know who the hell he was at that point – called me into an office and another guy came in wearing old clothes. Looked like he'd been pushing a broom in the backroom. I didn't know whether he was going to sweep under the chair or what.'

That man was Charles Marquis Warren, the show's producer, and keeping his cool, Clint casually asked him what the lead part was like. Warren replied there were two leads; one was a young guy in his early twenties – and that was the part they were interested in him for. 'So I started perking up, straightening out the wrinkles in my T-shirt, you know – I was just wearing levis – and finally the guy said, "Well, we'll get in touch with you." I kind of half-way wrote it off because I figured once they'd seen *Ambush*, that'd be the end of it.'

Clint left the studio after stopping by Sonia's desk to tell her about the meeting and went home to break the news to Maggie, trying to suppress his excitement about it. Later that afternoon, he got a call from Sparks to come back to the studio to make a test. 'I did that and another one the next morning. The big wheels at CBS liked it, and I was picked, and Eric Fleming was set as the other lead. That was a great day in my life; the money looked to me as if I'd be in a league with Howard Hughes!'

After all the hard work, the one-line bits, the rinky-dink studio classes, success was finally to drop into Eastwood's lap like an overripe orange falling into a passer-by's hand. It was the oldest story in Hollywood: being in the right place at the right time. For all his cool, it was luck, plain and simple, that had made the difference. The girl he stopped by to see that day and who worked as story editor on the series during it's long run is currently the story editor for Malpaso Productions – the company Eastwood now owns and which produces his films.

When he was putting Malpaso together, her name was one of the first on his list of possible crew members. She'd made a name for herself in television by creating the very successful series *Mr. Ed*, but she was eager to sign on. She's remained a friend of both Clint's and Maggie's and fits right into the family atmosphere he was seeking. Now she spends long hours searching out properties that can be tailored to the particular talents of her boss, a position she's so far filled with great success. She also enjoys being able to work among friends in one of the industry's most successful organisations.

The Rawhide *Years*

One thing about Clint Eastwood that's been true all his life is
that he knows a good thing when he sees it – or stumbles across
it like he did with *Rawhide*. Signing with CBS was the highest
watermark of his career, miles higher than the Universal deal
because this time he'd finally been accepted as an actor with
something specific to offer. He was determined to make it last
as long as he possibly could. He'd already waited too long for
it. The night he signed his deal with the network – he now had
an agent who took care of the details – was for him a night of
well-earned celebration, and he called his cronies from far and
wide to come and help him and Maggie celebrate. Their tiny
apartment in Studio City was quickly filled with the people
who'd helped him through the lean times. Everybody was
happy, and there were the usual cries of 'I knew it all along',
and 'It's always been only a matter of time for you, kid'. But
underneath all the surface noises was the satisfaction for all of
them it really *could* happen – just like that! One day you're
digging somebody else's swimming pool and the next day
you're out looking for somebody to dig one for you. It made
them all feel more hopeful because one of them had turned the
right handle, hit the right office, and now, hopefully, had
made it. They all felt that maybe *they* could make it too.

Television cowboys have never had much of a record for
longevity with the exception of a few like Matt Dillon, Wyatt
Earp and the *Mavericks*, Brett and Bart. In fact they're just
about the most fragile bird on the Hollywood tree despite their
super-masculine images. This fact has been proved countless
times when shows have been cancelled and the cowboy's
careers are suddenly over.

On the other end were the TV range riders who *did* make it;
successfully trading in their established small-screen image for

a chance at theatre screens and theatre screen-size money. In those days movie offers were more plentiful than now but there was still a slight stigma about being known as a television actor. In a town made of spun sugar dreams, a TV actor was on the bottom of the most-wanted list. James Garner had already made a few movies while still in his snap-brimmed black hat and white-vested, well-cut gambling suit as *Maverick*. Steve McQueen was itching to follow that same trail, but on the *Rawhide* set things were peaceful.

The contract was signed and filed for thirteen episodes which were well underway. As Rowdy Yates, Clint fitted the part and the saddle like they were second skin. The only rule the producers had laid down to him was to forget about haircuts for a while. He let his blond hair curl around his neck and ears – a style he wasn't crazy about personally, but which he knew worked for the character of Rowdy; and for the moment at least, Rowdy had the upper hand. After finishing ten of the contracted thirteen episodes, some bad news came from the front office. The word was out that hour-long Westerns were glutting the TV market and CBS's hopes for *Rawhide* had suddenly cooled. The production was shut down and temporarily shelved. It was a bitter pill for Clint to swallow. He'd thrown himself into the series with more energy than he'd ever used before as an actor.

'Here my career was, lying in the basement of CBS because the word was out that hour-long shows were finished. So I decided to go up and visit my parents – they had moved from Seattle back to Oakland by then – and Mag and I got on a train. On the way from Los Angeles to Oakland, I got a telegram saying the series had sold after all and to be ready to come back to work on such and such a day. So Mag and I did a little champagne trick and yelled a lot: I stuck my head out the window and shouted some profane things.'

The show premiered on the night of January 9th, 1959. When the reviews came in the next day, they were all good ones. More importantly, the show clicked with the viewers too, as the ratings demonstrated a few days later. *Rawhide* began a steady climb that quickly proved it was a hit.

Overnight Clint's status changed – he was finally and positively a star! Heady stuff for a guy who'd been knocking his head against the industry wall for years without a break. Unlike some others, however, Clint knew all too well that success can end just as abruptly as it starts. He'd been on unemployment lines with too many 'names' not to have learned that lesson. At twenty-eight Clint Eastwood had the wisdom of a man twice his age, and he wasn't about to let his ego forget the facts he had learned the hard way.

His thick crop of unruly blond hair quickly earned him the nickname 'Lionhead' on the set. He put up with it good-naturedly, but didn't really care for it. One of the first things he realised was that he should have taken the horseback-riding lessons a little more seriously when they'd been offered him at Universal. 'I wasn't much of a rider when I started *Rawhide*. I could stay on and that's about it. I hit the saddle pretty hard the first couple of weeks.' However, he found he really enjoyed it and began to think someday he'd even like to own a ranch, live there, and work it in his spare time.

His part didn't call for any great acting ability, but two average scripts were equal to all the lines of dialogue he'd had in almost his entire career up to that point. As he got better and better in the saddle, he asked the producers if he couldn't do a few of his own stunts. He found out, much to his surprise, that he was suddenly too valuable for that stuff any more. His fan mail had started coming in by the bagful, and the mailroom count convinced Charles Marquis Warren that Clint was too precious a commodity to risk injuring. Maggie continued working at modelling because she liked it, and it wasn't until *Rawhide* had been running a year or so that they decided to move from their small apartment to a small ranch house in Sherman Oaks, an exclusive section of Los Angeles where many other stars lived. It wasn't lavish, but there was room to move around, and to Clint, that was an important consideration.

The house reflected the interests of the couple who lived in it. Maggie had begun painting several years before, and her efforts dotted the walls alongside other paintings she'd collected. A pair of well-used surf-boards stood propped up in a corner near the new hi-fi, one of their few extravagances. In style it was basically California Comfortable with no pretensions to being anything other than the home of two uncomplicated people.

It was a place to relax, to entertain their friends, and to relax with each other. Clint built a barbeque in the backyard, which they used often. He also utilised the yard for his daily exercises. The surf-boards in the living-room weren't merely decorative. Clint made regular trips to the beach in even the coldest weather. Maggie usually joined him but begged off during the really cold months, preferring to stay home and work on a painting or other projects. There were no status symbols lying around – not even a swimming pool in the backyard. Clint and Maggie preferred the ocean.

Most of the interviews stressed two things about the up-and-coming TV cowboy. One was his happy home-life, the other was his healthy, direct approach to himself and his work. Admittedly, it didn't make them Hollywood's most exciting couple, but it was a refreshing change from the 'Now that I'm famous I'm unhappy' tales of other stars, which proliferated in the scandal magazines of that period.

TV Guide was one of the first magazines to do a piece on Eastwood. It was a straightforward interview, highlighting his health hints. Even today that publication doesn't venture into controversial areas, ever keeping in mind its primarily Middle-America readership. In 1961 it was primarily in the business of plumping up the American Dream. Clint stated that being a television star can make you lazy no matter on what side of the screen you happen to be. He advised parents to talk their kids into doing a few push-ups during the commercials. Photographed practising what he preached, between two collapsible deck-chairs in his backyard, he went on to say that, 'Walking and running are the best exercises if you can't get to a gymnasium or swimming pool. I work out Saturday mornings along the Los Angeles River with a friend. We run as hard as we can for a hundred yards, then walk for a hundred, then trot for a while, then walk again.' It was no secret that he believed the edge he had over a lot of other actors was his physique (Clint still takes great pride in how well he keeps in shape.) Universal had treated him like a piece of meat, and he believed that deep down you were only as good as you were healthy. 'A lot of actors,' he continued in the *TV Guide* interview, 'don't condition themselves to long periods of hard physical effort. Towards the end of the day it shows in their performances.' Besides that clue to what he felt about the competition, the article was basic fan magazine fodder, concluding with a list of his personal Do's and Don'ts of living.

Some *Do's*: 'Try to be optimistic; a bright outlook helps in everything. A discouraged attitude is a physical hindrance.

   'Eat fruits and raw vegetables like carrots, celery, cauliflower, lettuce and asparagus. You get the vitamins in their natural state.

   'Keep a scale in your bathroom and use it each morning. If you see the dial creeping over the figure you want, start watching your diet *that* day. A gradual increase in weight is hard to get rid of.'

Some *Don'ts*: 'The worst exercise you can get is with a knife and fork. Try to stay away from carbohydrates, especially rich desserts.

   'Avoid alcohol in excess.'

Tame stuff indeed! It was, nevertheless, valuable in steadily building his image as a good guy. The fact is that he personally believed every word of it!

Publicity also began establishing him as an actor who had *enjoyed* acting as a youngster, and to read it you'd think there was barely a community theatre anywhere in California whose boards he hadn't trod at least once. The drifting exploits of his early years were boiled down to a few lines which took him directly from San Francisco to Oakland, completely detouring around the many dusty stops, he'd made along the way.

But it was just part of the game. And so were the working

hours. *Rawhide* was filmed primarily on the MGM studio backlot, but sometimes on a location ranch about a hundred miles away. Clint spent many long hours commuting between the two places in his beat-up car. (His motorcycle was shelved for the duration of the shooting schedule.) A study in con- centration while on the set, he began building a reputation for clear-cut professionalism. He enjoyed working under clearly defined conditions, and he wasn't interested in rocking what was beginning to look like a very stable boat. He was a direc- tor's dream, and Ted Post, who directed some *Rawhide* seg- ments was to turn up later in Clint's career as director of two of his films. Again, the man in the saddle never forgot a buddy.

After the series got rolling, there was a parade of producers who were assigned to it over the seven-year run: some half- dozen in all. Clint appreciated them when they made things easier but was frank to admit that was rarely the case. He's never been overly fond of producers or other front-office men since then. He had a job to do and was happy to do it, with as few interruptions as possible. He especially disliked the memos that seemed to flow in a steady trickle from the faceless men in the big offices. They held up production and accomplished nothing.

As the series grew more and more popular he began to feel hemmed in, complaining to Maggie and finally to the press that the network didn't seem to be in any hurry to let him pick up on any of the star options that were a part of his contract. In July of 1961 he told Hank Grant of the *Hollywood Reporter* that he was fed up with the way he was being ignored by the front office and said point-blank exactly what he thought of it all: 'I haven't been allowed to accept a single feature or TV guesting offer since I started the series. Maybe they figure me as the sheepish nice guy I portray in the series, but even a worm has to turn sometime. Believe me,' he added, 'I'm not bluffing – I'm prepared to go on suspension, which means I can't work here, but I've got offers from London and Rome that'll bring me more money in a year than the series has given me in three.'

When that issue of the Hollywood trade paper – as much a

part of every exec's morning as his third cup of coffee – hit the desks at CBS, the telephones started ringing almost immediately. Clint the Co-operative? Clint the Unflappable, making statements like this? Who'd have thought it? Obviously the man meant business. It's typical of Eastwood that he would go along saying nothing for a long time, but that when he did decide to speak out, he'd do it in the simplest, most effective way. It's his old habit of never having to say a thing twice.

Shortly thereafter he began making the talk show rounds. Though he is now disenchanted with such methods, he still occasionally appears on them to plug a new movie. His agent let it be known that Big Clint was available for a feature film during the series layoff time several months a year. The producers also began to give him a little more latitude in the part of Rowdy, and he began experimenting a bit with acting styles and deliveries.

He and some friends were planning a production of a French farce for a Hollywood little theatre group. He was quick to explain to those who listened in total disbelief that, 'We'd only do it for a couple of weeks – just for laughs.' It never jelled, which was probably just as well, but the notion was there. Another, less surprising idea was that he'd like to try another kind of out-of-the saddle role, '... something that might get me away from Westerns. I don't mean I'm a drawing-room actor or anything like that, but I always wanted to wear my hair in a crew cut, and it would be kind of nice to get it back again. They tell me the guys really did wear their hair long like this in the old trail days, but I don't see how they stood it. I would have shaved mine off as close as I could get it. Darn stuff picks up more dirt!'

Few people remember it now, but there was also a time when Clint Eastwood was on the verge of being a singer. A fact forgotten even by the producers of *Paint Your Wagon*, until he reminded them of it. On a *Rawhide* episode he warbled a song about the lonesome trail, the lonesome pines and the lonesome saddle that sent scores of TV fans to their ballpoint pens to dash off letters asking for more of the same. In those days there was hardly a cowboy who *didn't* sing. Thirteen of them then riding the TV range had at least one record under their belt. Clint made a deal with a company called Gothic Records and made his first – and last – single for them, *Unknown Girl*, backed with *For All We Know*. He got it out of his system but is reminded of it when a playful Maggie unearths one of the scratched copies and spins it for him.

The bare facts of his publicity bios paint a clear picture of a conservative man whose tastes in just about everything couldn't alienate anybody. His favourite singers were Nat King Cole and Frank Sinatra with the distaff side held down by Peggy Lee and Ella Fitzgerald. Hobbies included surfing, water skiing, golf, swimming and that staple of the fan profile, collecting records. His favourite instrument is listed as the piano, and his favourite foods as steak, lobster and spaghetti.

In short he was the All-American boy, willing and able to appeal to every viewer. That network-approved synopsis of his likes and dislikes is the closest Clint has ever come to the then-mandatory 'I love everybody' publicity attitude especially important to television personalities. People weren't going out to pay money to see TV stars but were instead having them into their homes once a week (hopefully). There was no room for controversy. Even the long hair was apologised for at length.

Clint was proud of his work and proud of the series because he felt it was an honest testament to the Old West. 'I mean we're doing stories as they pretty much happened. Oh, occasionally I guess we hoke one up for dramatic purposes, but generally speaking we're doing the things that guys on the cattle drives really did.'

Clint was also proud of his star status, and whenever he got a script that played Fleming more than himself, he'd be off to the producer to straighten it out. Luckily Warren, who throughout the show's run kept close tabs on it, thought Clint's contributions to the proceedings at least equal to his complaints. Once he even considered making the show a completely alternating star vehicle with Fleming on top one week and Clint the next. 'That'll keep 'em both happy,' he sighed more than once.

On the set Clint remained a model of comportment, and his disputes with Fleming, never major, were handled through the channels the studio set up for such things. Onscreen they complemented each other, contrasting as perfectly as the producers had originally hoped they would. Fleming's bullet-biting delivery and Eastwood's amiability blended well. Between takes on MGM's Stage 22 they often shared a joke or a beer when Clint wasn't exercising or giving interviews in the slightly apologetic manner that became a trademark. A Hollywood sage remarked that the name Rowdy fits Eastwood about as well as Pollyanna would fit Alfred Hitchcock.

Clint does have a temper, however, and there are times when it has to be dealt with. Once, when he was on a promotional trip to Indianapolis over Memorial Day in 1961, a girl walked over to his table in a night-club and poured a drink over his head. After seething a moment or two, he sprang from his chair and chased her out of the place, grabbing drinks from the tables he passed and flinging them at his assailant. She just managed to make it to her car before he was calmed down by a network aide assigned to watch out for him. There was now *one* viewer who knew that when irked enough Clint was Rowdy indeed!

A Fistful of Dollars

Despite the network's O.K. for Clint to use his lay-off time to make a feature film, his announcement of it didn't exactly bring a downpour of offers. Producers still thought that TV stars, with rare exceptions, were strictly that and even with the dramatic changeovers of James Garner and Steve McQueen from the small screen on to the big one, they weren't convinced Clint could make the same trip.

It wasn't until the spring of 1964 that his agent got a call from a harried director in Rome named Sergio Leone who was ready to roll on a Western to be filmed in Spain. Leone didn't have a star. He'd got Clint's name from muscle-man Richard Harrison who was then enjoying great popularity as an Italian version of Errol Flynn. Leone wanted to know if Clint was available. When the agent passed along the information that it was an Italian/Spanish/German/Western to be made in Spain with an Italian cast, Clint's first reaction was to laugh it off as a joke. But his agent had promised he'd at least have him read the script, which was being sent from Rome, and asked Clint to read it as a favour to him. Clint, after reading it, deliberated briefly and decided to make the picture. He recognised the plot as being the same one used in a Japanese film he'd admired called *Yojimbo*. It was directed by Akira Kurosawa. In fact, he and a friend had once remarked how good a Western it would make, perhaps inspired by the success of another Japanese-derived blockbuster *The Magnificent Seven* which Kurosawa had made originally as *The Seven Samurai*.

'Although the dialogue was atrocious, I could see that it was intelligently laid out. I said to Mag, who hadn't seen *Yojimbo*, "Read this and tell me what you think of it." And she read it and said "Wow, it's really interesting. It's wild." So I told the agent "O.K., go ahead. I've really got nothing to lose on this deal because if the picture bombs, it won't go anywhere." And I had a hunch that if it was handled well, it'd work.' That was a recent statement how *Fistful of Dollars* first came about and contains perhaps an enlarged dose of hindsight. When Clint finished shooting the picture, he returned home and promptly forgot all about it. Sometime later, a newsman travelling in Europe learned of the sensation it was causing at the box office there and brought the news back to Eastwood.

There is no doubt the character of the lonely drifter appealed greatly to Clint. He was getting a bit tired of the squeaky-clean image of Rowdy Yates who rode into the country's living-rooms every week with nary a trace of sweat or grime to show for it. He also noted the undeniable kinship between his own life and The Man With No Name. Hadn't he felt just like him any number of times during those growing-up years of movement and rootlessness? The minute this character appears on screen you wonder where he's been, what he's done. You meet him in the middle of a journey that's already made him come alive without a word of establishing dialogue.

'I wanted something earthier. Something different from the old-fashioned Western. You know, hero rides in, very stalwart with white hat; man's beating a horse; hero jumps off, punches man; schoolmarm walks down the street, sees this situation going on; slight conflict between hero and schoolmarm, but not too much. You know schoolmarm and hero will be together in exactly ten more reels, if you care to sit around and wait, and you know man who beats horse will eventually get come-uppance from hero when this guy bushwhacks him in reel nine. But this film was different; it definitely had satiric overtones. The hero was an enigmatic figure, and that worked within the context of this picture. In some films he would be ludicrous. You can't have a cartoon in the middle of a Renoir.'

After a couple of noteworthy stop-offs at a Western clothes shop on Hollywood Boulevard where he bought some black levis, and a cigar store in Beverly Hills where he stocked up on the small black stogies that were soon a stock part of the character's image, Clint packed his boots and gunbelt from *Rawhide* and flew to Spain. A non-smoker in real life, he smoked the cigars in the picture for effect only, a carefully gauged bit of action that was to become one of the character's trademarks. 'I didn't really like them, but they kept me in the right kind of humour. Kind of a fog.'

The picture was budgeted at a modest, even at European standards, $200,000, with fifteen of that going to Clint as the star. (He's since said he decided to make the picture because it included a free trip to Europe.) The supporting cast was all European although initially, before the Spaghetti Western was to make its own kind of history, this was partially disguised with American names. Clint's co-star and chief villain of the picture was billed as Johnny Wels, or Welles, but was in reality Gian Maria Volonte, one of Italy's most respected actors. Volonte went on to star in *Investigation of a Citizen Above Suspicion* in 1970. Other noteworthy name changes were Leone himself who emerged as Bob Robertson and composer Ennio Morricone, dubbed Don Savio. (The 'Spaghetti Westerns' are usually located in the Texas–Mexico border area to help the Mediterranean-looking cast appear more convincing. In many of the follow-ups, directors like Luigi Vanzi became Vance Lewis, Giorgio Ferroni was changed to Calvin Jackson Paget, while actor Giuliano Gemma – one of Italy's biggest stars – became Montgomary Wood and Ida Galli became Evelyn Stewart.)

European moviemakers were no strangers to the Western genre, having been producing their own versions of the American epics since the Twenties. Up to that point, though, they were mostly shoddy imitations for the home market in the tried-and-true vein of the good guy versus the bad guy as in the German productions of the James Fenimore Cooper tales mentioned earlier.

Leone was so personally enamoured of the genre he even affected Western clothes himself. He had in mind a new twist he wanted to give his heroes. Clint Eastwood was his prototype and most successful realisation. The most basic reason for the ultimate screen effect of stark sparseness was: there wasn't any extra money to gloss things over! The location of Almeria, Spain was as desolate as any that could be found, and therefore the cheapest to use. The tight shooting schedule of nine weeks left little room for retakes, which moved the naturally histrionic Spanish and Italian actors to give all they had in the first take.

Eastwood's larger-than-life character, over the years has attained almost god-like proportions in the amount of frenzied imitators he's inspired. Leone left Clint to do a lot of the character delineation himself and accepted both the black levis, carefully bleached out by now to a filthy grey, and the cigars. One reason for this blanket acceptance was that Leone couldn't speak English. 'Sergio and I got along fine. Of course, at first, we couldn't converse much; he spoke absolutely no English and my Italian was just *ciao* and *arrivederci*, and that was about it. So I did my own thing, and he did his. He speaks better English now, and I speak a little better Italian. I suppose we got together somewhere during our second picture.'

Since time was so limited for shooting the picture and Leone had so much tied up in it – the arrangement of the triple production company alone had been an exhausting feat – he was adamant about telling the producers that Clint was doing exactly what he wanted him to do. They told him they didn't like Eastwood's one-dimensional characterisation which was coming across in the daily rushes. To Clint he simply said *bene bene*, or roughly translated, 'keep going', and directed his other cast members to give an ever broader interpretation to their parts than they had been giving. It was a gamble, but the pieces fit together like the shards of an ancient plate on which was painted a travesty of traditional heroes and villains. It covered all the shades of black from the light-grey of a mercenary heart to the pit-like darkness of vengeance and murder.

When shooting was completed, both in Spain and at Rome's Cinecitta Studios, Clint returned home for another season on *Rawhide*. After a quick shave he was right back to being Rowdy Yates. However, he'd left behind in Italy a new Eastwood, a tight-lipped, poncho-wrapped protagonist who was ultimately to make him one of the most popular stars in the world.

The film opened in Naples, where it played to an audience of about fifty people. But the word-of-mouth of those fifty soon mushroomed to overflow crowds, and Leone knew he had struck the right combination. His gamble had worked, and his first thought was to expand it a bit and try again. He started working on a sequel, *For A Few Dollars More*, which he offered to Clint for shooting during his next TV lay-off, the summer of '65. By then Eastwood realised he had a good thing going too. His agent negotiated a deal whereby he'd be paid $50,000, and few more star-like fringe benefits – among them a bright red Ferrari to take back home with him.

The success of *Fistful of Dollars* enabled Leone to ask for more money to put the second picture together. His budget this time was $600,000 – three times that of the first. He was therefore able to afford another star, Lee Van Cleef. Van Cleef, an American actor who'd been commuting to Europe for years, was just about to come into his own as a full-fledged box-office attraction. The hero/villain Leone part fitted right in with his plans. (After the success of *For A Few Dollars More*, he was able to write his own ticket in the Spaghetti Western field and starred solo in several, including *Sabata*. He joined stars like Jim Brown in *El Condor* and John Philip Law in *Death Rides A Horse*.)

Again Eastwood was The Man With No Name, complete with flea-bitten poncho and stubby cigar, who joins up with Van Cleef as the Colonel, in pursuit of a mad killer with a price on his head. The killer, Indio, was again played by Gian Maria Volonte, this time under his real name. Though Van Cleef is interested in finding the man for personal revenge, it's plain all Eastwood is interested in is the reward money, some $10,000.

Leone's triangular struggle of rivalry is brought into sharp focus as the three characters fight each other every step of the way, each intent on his own purpose: money, revenge and escape. The score, again by Morricone, surpassed the one he'd composed for *Fistful*. It became an integral part of the action, particularly at the film's end when Eastwood stands with a circular watch, counting down music-punctuated seconds, the final note of which is the signal for the Colonel and Indio to draw.

Though the critics thought no better of *For A Few Dollars*

More than they did of *Fistful*, it is a vastly superior film. The direction is more detailed and the pacing of the action more calculated.

One of the directors who'd been most impressed with Clint in *Fistful* was Vittorio De Sica, the great post-war Italian genius. He wanted Clint for a movie of his own. After shooting ended on *For A Few Dollars More*, Clint went to Rome to listen to De Sica's proposition. The twelve-week shooting schedule had about exhausted his time free from *Rawhide*, but Clint was interested. De Sica's offer was that of the male lead in an episode of a new film being produced by the Italian Cecil B. DeMille – Dino De Laurentiis.

De Laurentiis was at the time one of Italy's most prolific moviemakers, but he was also, and still is, very much married to Sylvana Mangano, the lush actress who first attracted international attention in the early Fifties in *Bitter Rice*. Mangano had ripened into a mature beauty, and Dino managed her career much as Carlo Ponti managed that of his wife Sophia Loren. He shepherded her from picture to picture, notably the top-heavy historical drama of *Barrabas* which had also starred Anthony Quinn. Unlike Loren, however, Sylvana's career had never taken off in the international arena as her husband had hoped. He was sure his latest project, *The Witches*, would do the trick. She'd been off the screen a few years and the multi-episode film was calculated to show all her varied talents. There were five different directors on the project. De Sica was directing the last one, called '*A Night Like Any Other*', and he wanted Clint for this film.

Undoubtedly De Sica hoped to plug into Clint's popularity, but that was not to be the case. The sequence was a contemporary fantasy with Sylvana lavishly costumed in head-dresses and silks while Clint lounged around looking decidedly out of place. Away from his now-familiar costume of scruffy serape and weeks-old beard, he seemed a bit lost. He wandered amiably through his scenes with a blank stiffness and remained classically handsome, but not very exciting. De Sica had called him the new Gary Cooper and must have been heartily disappointed.

Four years later, just to make sure no one else would cash in on the film, United Artists imported it to America, but it got only modest distribution in out-of-the-way art houses and was quickly shelved. So far it hasn't even shown up on television – that restless graveyard of unsuccessful films. Clint himself has stopped mentioning it altogether. The last time he spoke of it was offhandedly in the Sixties when he said of his part, 'It was a drawing-room thing, half reality, half fantasy. It was good to get out of my boots though.'

Maggie was in Rome at this time, and together they had their first real chance to gauge Clint's rising stardom. *A Fistful of Dollars* was the sensation of the year, and the Italian movie industry at large was on its collective knees to the American who singlehandedly seemed to be pumping new life into it. When the Eastwoods dined out, the reaction from the public was hysterical (but at least Clint got a chance to sample Italy's beer – a hobby he pursues wherever his work takes him). It was the tail end of *La Dolce Vita* time in Rome, but Clint and Maggie couldn't tell that from the reception they got. Papparazzi followed them like flies after a hunk of raw meat, and they provided a kind of adulation that had long since died at home. Things were happening fast.

Returning home to their three-quarter acre hillside in Holly-wood, they carried with them the excitement they'd so recently tasted on the Via Veneto. Clint told Sheilah Graham, then the ranking Hollywood gossip columnist, 'I'm probably the highest paid American actor who ever worked in Italian pictures.' Negotiations had been completed before he'd left Rome for still another Western to be made the next summer, and his salary for that one had shot up to a quarter of a million dollars plus 10 per cent of the Western hemisphere profits. Even now he retains a hefty percentage of profits from all his pictures that play in Italy, which he calls his good-luck country. Not one of them has ever flopped there. 'Only Mastroianni gets more in Italy,' he added happily. 'I've been offered several Westerns in America, but I've turned them all down because they are not very good. I don't want to make all my Westerns in Italy and Spain, but in Europe I'm in a better position to get the films I want and to work with people like De Sica. I passed up a picture in London, a James Bond type. For the first time in my life, I can pick the parts I want to play.'

He recalled that when he first considered going to Universal he was told to dye his hair black because 'they go for Rock Hudson types at Universal. At 20th Century Fox you can have light hair.' It was easy to see that his memory of those months hadn't faded a bit in the ensuing years. But Clint prefers looking ahead, and in 1966 was quoted as saying, 'Rome is like a village. Working there is a family-like thing. Everyone joins in and volunteers to help. It's not as businesslike or cold as in America.'

Over on the *Rawhide* set there had been some serious changes made during his absence that quickly worked out to his advantage. Though his reputation was preceding him, his movies hadn't reached the United States yet, so to CBS he was still just another contract star, albeit a rising one. Eric Fleming had got the big studio call while Clint was away and had gone to MGM to star with Doris Day in *The Glass Bottom Boat*. He'd been dropped from *Rawhide* because of this, and suddenly Clint found himself in the top spot on the show. But this time, however, viewers had lost some of their enthusiasm for that seemingly endless cattle drive to Sedalia, Missouri – the destination he and Fleming started out for seven years earlier (Fleming died in 1966 on location in Perp for an MGM-TV series, *High Jungle*. He drowned in the Amazon.)

During Clint's absence, network chief James Aubrey had cancelled the series because of its faltering ratings, but was then himself cancelled by CBS, and the series was again put into a 'go' position for its eighth season. Network support was still shaky, however, and finally the decision to cancel it once and for all came in midseason with seventeen episodes left to be filmed. The trail ride was over for Eastwood, but he cashed in his saddle and spurs for a $119,000 cash settlement with CBS on February 8th, 1966. He was a free man, and his third Italian picture was reassigned to start in May to take advantage of his changed schedule. It was to be called *The Magnificent Rogues*, and the money he was getting for it seemed to him a clear barometer that things were going straight up for him.

Leone had broken up his original production triumvirate Jolly/Ocean/Constantin Films after *Fistful* was completed. Jolly Films brought out a picture entitled *The Magnificent Stranger* (the original title of *Fistful*) under their own banner, billing it as a new Clint Eastwood Western. It was a blend of two old *Rawhide* segments the company had purchased and to which they'd attempted to add colour. When Clint heard of it, he sued and the picture was soon withdrawn. It was not an uncommon practice at the time, and series like *The Man From U.N.C.L.E.* have often had various episodes surface in Europe as feature movies.

The following year it was tried again by another small company called Lucas Films, but at least this attempt to cash in on Clint's name had a little style. The company headlined in trade papers that 'Clint Eastwood is proud to announce his new film *El Gringero,* to be released in September in colour and directed by Clarence Brown'. Brown of course, was one of the most famous American 'class' directors of the Thirties who shepherded Greta Garbo through many of her films: he also knew nothing of the film. Another case of intercutting television film, *El Gringero* was quickly dropped and it's doubtful if Clint even had a chance to see it.

Leone had set up a deal with United Artists for his third Spaghetti Western with Eastwood under his own production banner, P.E.A. Films. He wrote the screenplay himself along with Luciano Vincenzoni and set up a cast to include Lee Van Cleef with Eli Wallach in the pivotal role of Tuco, the Mexican bandit. He also changed the title of the film to *The Good, The Bad and The Ugly* with Eastwood roughly the Good, Eli Wallach the Bad and Van Cleef, the Ugly. The most ambitious of his three Westerns, Leone had a budget six times greater than the one for *Fistful of Dollar*s – $1,200,000, and while Clint's character Joe technically had a name in the script, he was basically once again The Man With No Name: a stranger who interjects himself into the action for a piece of it!

This third part of Leone's violent trilogy gave the genre he'd created a respectability born of sheer popularity. What had been dismissed three years earlier at the Naples opening of *Fistful* as 'not being worth a lira' had proved itself worth many millions of them. Leone was supplying the most popular commodity on the screen, and its cornerstone was Stoic Clint, the stranger in a world of evil and unrelenting violence who wanders through looking for a profitable way out.

Why has he never done another film with Leone? Probably the easiest answer to that is he's advanced beyond the limitations of Leone's original conception. Leone himself has carried his own creation further and further with pictures like *Duck, You Sucker* and *Once Upon A Time In The West*. He continues to expand his basic theme of man's need to survive, no matter how unreal and perverse the world he finds himself in. Means are unimportant; if he survives, he's a winner. If he dies, no matter how bravely, he's a loser. It was a winning combination for Eastwood.

Hail the
Reconquering Hero

The start of 1967 saw the *Dollar* films, as the three Eastwood Westerns have been called, looming like a storm over the Atlantic getting ready to crash over the United States. The legal complications over the rights to the plot of *Fistful of Dollars* were nearing a settlement. Leone never purchased *Yojimbo* rights for the United States, and subsequently the picture couldn't be shown here until the legal owners were satisfied. That took some doing after they saw what a moneymaker it was. United Artists controlled both *Fistful* and the two follow-up films for release here.

When it did open in February (during a blizzard), it got a critical crucifixion for its excessive violence but proved an exhibitor's delight as a groundswell of support quickly made it a hit. Poster shops were suddenly stocked with a new addition. A picture of a sneering Clint wrapped in the serape of The Man With No Name, his face in shadow from the flat-topped black hat and his mouth clenched around an unlit cheroot. In only a few weeks it took its place as a top seller alongside one of a youthful Steve McQueen on a motorcycle, Clark Gable as Rhett Butler casually fanning a hand of poker, a pouting Marilyn Monroe, and a languid Hedy Lamarr stretched out as Tondelayo in *White Cargo*. It was instant camp but it was also a clear barometer of instant success in the frenzied counter culture of the psychedelic Sixties.

Just prior to its release, Clint had been in New York doing an interview with William Peper of the now-defunct World-Journal Tribune, and they'd gone to dinner at the chic Sherry Netherland Hotel. To the other diners in the room Clint was just another vaguely familiar face from the TV screen, but when the maître d' (who'd just arrived in New York from Italy) approached them, it was a very different story. 'Clint

Eastwood!' he gasped before lapsing into a spate of enthusiastic Italian, 'My wife see your picture three times. My son five times.' Proof enough for Peper that Clint's love affair with the Italians wasn't just a press release idea.

Critics who unwillingly flocked to Eastwood for interviews – most of them hated the picture yet couldn't ignore him in light of its success – found a changed man from the old days of Rowdy Yates. There was a power which had been absent before, a strong sense of self, and a clear perspective on his own contributions in making his picture a hit. It was at once formidable and understandable. Women especially found his new status intriguing. Comments on The Man With No Name such as 'he's raunchy, not very gallant', and 'when he does a nice deed, he doesn't bend over backward to take credit for it' had a deeper meaning when they researched his private life and found his movie image closely paralleled his own.

Naturally his series was mentioned, and he was frankly grateful for it. 'I had *Rawhide* for seven years. I learned that TV builds you for immediate stardom, and when your show closes or starts to fade, it takes it away like chocolate from a kid. But I was lucky. I had *Fistful*.' While willing to acknowledge the debt he owed television (Leone has since admitted he first saw Eastwood on American television in the *Rawhide* series and remembered him when his name came up for *Fistful*), he was in no mood to consider crossing back over the line from the large screen to the small. 'A film is easier to do,' he explained, 'It pays better and gives you more credit and prestige.' Of the Man With No Name he said briefly, 'I like the idea of a lead who thinks only of what's in it for him.' The poncho trademark was suddenly his idea too – 'I happened to have one with me.' Again he plugged the realism of the film. 'When I get beaten up, which I do a lot, it takes me time to mend. I don't just go to the river and wash off the bruises.'

For A Few Dollars More was released in the summer of '67 and continued his winning streak, but the accompanying avalanche of publicity did little to change his lifestyle. He was smart enough to know that even a good product benefits from the personal touch and agreed to go to Europe on a promotion tour, taking Maggie with him. During a New York stopover he joked to one reporter that 'She's seen more of Europe than I have. She'll come in and do the tours (during shooting of a film) while all I get to see is myself on horseback looking at a sunset.' He also noted he was getting better at the interviewing game – the French wanted to dissect his stardom and the Italians, his marriage!

Before they left for Europe though, Clint began work on a dream he'd sidelined for years. He purchased a large tract of mountainous land on the Monterey Peninsula outside Carmel. It's rugged land but awesomely beautiful and has been a favourite hideout for stars like Kim Novak and Jean Arthur over the years. His idea was the same as theirs – privacy – but as usual he'd waited until he could do it *his* way. There was already a small house on the property, which they moved into while they began laying out the plans for the new house. Clint held on to the house in Sherman Oaks for those periods when he was stuck in town. Several years before, he'd added a fully equipped gym to the floor over the garage and when there, spent at least an hour a day lifting weights and using a punching bag. 'All,' said Maggie, 'to keep his machinery in shape.'

But the 200-acre spread also had a stretch of beach, and it was that he was looking forward to getting back to. Although he admitted he wasn't exactly a pro in the hammer-and-nails department, Clint said he wanted to do as much of the work as possible. One of the first orders he gave for the house was for oversized bathtubs – a fetish of his after years of cramming his 6 ft. 4 in. frame into regular-sized ones.

Surprisingly, with all his new-found fame, Clint was not besieged with scripts from the Hollywood studios. The up-front men had him pegged as an ex-TV star who'd got a little lucky on the other side, and they didn't seem in any hurry to change their thinking. United Artists knew better and offered him the script *Hang 'Em High*. Admittedly the plot was a carbon copy of the Spaghetti Westerns, but it was a good one: fast, violent and honest. They had a cast lined up which included Ed Begley, Pat Hingle, Alan Hale, J., Ben Johnson, plus three younger actors, James MacArthur, Bruce Dern and

Dennis Hopper (just before his *Easy Rider* success). Shooting was scheduled to be mostly on location in New Mexico. Again Clint was the angry loner, but this time he was out to seek revenge on the men who had hanged him and left him for dead. With almost classical poetic justice, he searches and finds them one by one, despatching them to their just reward.

So confident was United Artists that it would be a winner, they didn't hesitate in paying Clint a staggering $400,000 for doing the picture, plus 25 per cent of the net profits. Ted Post, one of *Rawhide*'s many directors, was getting his first crack at a major feature film with this one, and the result paid off for United Artists. *Hang 'Em High* made back its entire production cost and went into the money in a phenomenal ten weeks: the fastest payoff in the studio's history.

Second-billed behind Clint was Inger Stevens, and the pair became close friends during the shooting of the picture. As the love-starved rape victim unable to return his admiration she demonstrated the talent that had made her a durable actress and also bits of the personal heartbreak which, months later, would result in her death by suicide. Clint is always quick to say that her performance helped give the picture just the right touch of humanity which added to its overall success.

Its instant-hit status convinced Hollywood producers that Clint was more than just a flash in an Italian frying pan, and offers for his services came flooding into his agent's office, accompanied by a small avalanche of scripts. There were so many that his business manager, the late Irving Leonard, suggested it would be wise for him to form his own company. Clint took this good advice and Malpaso Productions was born. Malpaso means 'bad step' – Clint apparently isn't superstitious – and it was named after a creek that flowed through the Eastwood Monterey property.

Overnight Clint became one of the busiest men in the business. Taking an interest in every deal that was offered, he spent hours reading scripts and putting together the tight personal organisation that has allowed him more control and latitude over his career than practically any other star in the business. He opened his mind to the reservoir of information he'd stored up over the years while at Universal and later on countless TV sets, and channeled it into his new company. His motto was economy: economy of words, of production money, and of energy, suddenly his most vital asset. No lavish offices were established – not even a door that said Clint Eastwood, President. He owns the controlling stock but views himself simply as the company's principal commodity for hire.

The first attractive nibble for his services came, ironically, from Universal, the studio that had dumped him in 1956. They came to him with an unfinished script about a modern-day Arizona lawman who goes to New York to arrange the extradition of a criminal and for the first time faces the insecurities of being off his home ground. It was to be a complete change of pace for him, and it's likely there was a good deal of head-shaking about taking him off the range where he'd roped in millions already. But he was ready to take the chance. And why not? Things had never been better for him, and most excitingly perhaps, was the news that Maggie was pregnant after nearly fourteen years of marriage! The anticipation he felt about becoming a father just added to his self-confidence.

The picture they had in mind was to be called *Coogan's Bluff* and was to mark more than one turning point for Clint. It brought him into contact with the man who has had the most to do with his continued success – director Don Siegel. As Clint tells it, 'Universal had lined up a director named Alex Siegel for the project but when he dropped out we were looking for another one. When Don's name came up, they said I was "warm" in Italy, and he was "warm" in France, so maybe the two of us would get along. I went looking at some of the films he'd done, a couple of television shows and the movie *The Killers*, and I was very impressed.' Siegel himself says he thinks their getting together was basically a computer error: 'It's true about Alex Seigel and, also, he was considering a very good director, Don Taylor (a movie star in the late Forties and early Fifties), and I think the computer got it all confused and it came out Don Siegel! The other thing was that when I was told about the project – I knew he'd run one of my pictures – I said, "Well I want to run some of his pictures" – I felt like an idiot – and I ran the three Leone pictures. Really super films, and I said "fine", but that wasn't good enough so I called a meeting, thinking that would kill it. I went up to Carmel, thought I was going to play a little golf, he took one look at me and we went to work.'

Siegel had a career in Hollywood that dated back to the early Thirties. He'd been assistant film librarian at Warner Bros., slowly graduating over the years through the Montage Department (which he created) and into wartime documentary films, one of which, *Hitler Lives*, won an Academy Award in 1945. He directed his first feature for them in '46, called *The Verdict*, and has since made such films as the classic science fiction *Invasion of the Body Snatchers*, in addition to contemporary statements like *Riot in Cell Block Eleven*, *The Big Steal* and *Crime In The Streets* among others. His unstintingly violent exposés of the human condition and his virtual creation of the anti-hero figure has led to a cult-like following in Europe. At home he was considered a competent, low-budget director who brought in violence when he ran low on story line.

For years he'd had the reputation that he didn't like actors who thought too much – especially about what was going on in front of the camera. Yet both he and Clint were able to work out a viable compromise that profited both of them. Clint had begun thinking of directing himself in a picture and was not over-shy on offering Siegel observations he'd gleaned over the years from his own experiences. 'Clint has very good ideas about setups and things, and I call them Clintus shots. Now I'll try to figure out a shot to top it and if I do it's called a Siegelini shot. It's not any big deal but many times his ideas will lead me into another channel of thought, and I'll come up with a new approach. Certainly I know whether it's better. If it isn't, then I don't use it. But he's not suggesting it in any other way than to simply add and make better what we're doing. It's a peculiar relationship. He doesn't treat me as the producer or director and I don't treat him as the star, *and* my boss – I'm working for his company! What we're trying to do is to tell a story as well as we can.'

Siegel had formed his own opinion of Clint by the time the

first camera rolled and it's an interesting mixture of ideas. On the one hand he feels Clint is closer than anyone currently on the screen to the hero image of Gary Cooper, and yet he recognises Eastwood's transformation into the ultimate anti-hero. 'Clint has an absolute fixation as an anti-hero,' he once told *Films and Filming*. 'It's his credo in life and in all the films that he's done so far. And it has been very successful, certainly for Clint and for those who own a piece of his pictures. He insists on being an anti-hero. I've never worked with an actor who was less conscious of his good image.'

He played upon this in his direction of Clint as Walt Coogan, an instinctive hunter who functions best in the wilds and alone. When he's talked into going to New York to track down an escaped killer, he immediately runs afoul of the system, and the basic story is how he combats it to do his job. It was filmed on location in Arizona and New York, where for the final chase sequence the film company was able to get permission to use *The Cloisters*. It's unlikely that ever in its history has that gift of William Randolph Hearst seen the likes of such goings-on. Coogan corners Ringerman, played by Don Stroud, in a shoot-out that ends in a motorcycle duel on the former Benedictine priory's steps.

For the first time critics began to see there was something lurking beneath Clint's grim exterior besides latent hostility, and it had taken Siegel to bring it out. The picture was a success and Clint wanted to work with Don again as soon as possible. Malpaso had already lined him up for three films, however, and they didn't get together again until *Two Mules For Sister Sara* in 1970. The character he played in *Coogan* got a name change and a little whitewash when it was transformed into TV's *McCloud* series starring Dennis Weaver.

The first of the contracted films that Malpaso loaned him out for was *Where Eagles Dare*, a World War II action drama about eight international adventurers – seven men and one woman – who attempt to infiltrate a Nazi-held castle in the Alps in order to free an Allied officer held captive there. Clint, as an American Ranger named Lt. Morris Schaffer, is once again an outsider who joins the group in the twisting screenplay written by Alistair MacLean. Richard Burton, as John Smith, supplies the brains behind the operation, but Clint contributes the American savvy that helps them pull the operation off.

It was the first time in his renewed career that Clint took second billing and second money, but the cast lineup and obvious commercial prospects of the film made it valuable. Burton got $1,200,000 against Clint's $800,000, but it was a chance at a new kind of exposure. He also added another starring role to the project, buttressing Burton's fading reputation as a ticket seller.

Basically it was a tongue-in-cheek epic, totally unbelievable, but with enough action to keep all his fans happy. He also became good friends with Burton and then-wife Elizabeth Taylor. Those were the days when Elizabeth accompanied her husband to every film location, no matter how remote, and there was plenty of chance for the three to get acquainted during the shooting in the Austrian Alps. When Liz wasn't sitting on the sidelines of the set itself, visiting with co-star Mary Ure, or writing numerous letters to her children, she read some of the scripts that were constantly coming to her.

Maggie was home waiting the birth of their first child. During some small talk with Liz, the subject inevitably turned to him and Liz doing a movie together. She was vastly impressed by his good looks and quiet charm and thought that onscreen they'd be dynamite together if, that is, she ever decided to do a Western. What started out as a joke soon looked like reality when she came to him with one of the scripts she'd been sent, something called *Two Mules For Sister Sara*, a frontier *African Queen*, which she thought might be just the ticket. When he read it, Clint agreed that it had possibilities and forwarded it on to Malpaso who set up a deal with Universal to produce it with Clint and Liz when both their schedules permitted.

Clint's son was born May 19th, 1968 and that news was worth celebrating, especially on a location where even the morning mail was a big event. Before he left for *Eagles*, Clint and Maggie talked about what they'd call the baby if it was a boy and one thing Clint was adamant about was that he wouldn't be Clinton III. He felt strongly that the child should have his own name and his own identity. Maggie wanted to call the baby after him, but Clint stuck to his guns. He left it up to her to come up with another name. She decided on Kyle. That was O.K. with Clint, so when he got home he was introduced to his son, Kyle Clinton Eastwood. Maggie communicated with Clint regularly and he learned that construction of the Carmel house had been started and that it was to be built partly of redwood timbers that had once been used to support several Monterey bridges. He preferred that to cutting down new trees.

When shooting was completed, the cast, crew and assorted family and friends of the *Eagles* cast moved intact to England's Borehamwood Studios where interiors were to be shot. It was wound up quickly and Clint said his good-byes to everybody, including his friends Liz and Dick, promising to keep in touch with Elizabeth about their picture. Once home, however, he barely had time to shake his tiny son's hand before re-packing his bag to set out for Oregon for five months of location shooting on the musical, *Paint Your Wagon*. This was a co-production of lyricist Alan Jay Lerner, Clint's Malpaso, and Paramount Pictures. Paramount was footing the bills for what they hoped would be a glorious return of the movie musical. *Wagon*, one of Broadway's greatest hits, seemed like a natural for transition to the silver screen.

Malpaso was making a small fortune loaning Clint to star in the epic musical and it seemed like a sure-fire winner. Lee Marvin and Jean Seberg were to co-star with Clint along with Harve Presnell, Ray Walston, and Tom Ligon, a young actor from Broadway in his first major film. The budget was a huge one (Paramount was sparing no expense that year with musicals, having just bankrolled Julie Andrews in the costly *Darling Lily* with Rock Hudson) and veteran director Joshua Logan was signal to whip the team into shape.

For Clint, the project got off to a bumpy start. The first day of shooting on the Paramount lot, he showed up in his pick-up truck (which he'd had equipped with air-conditioning and a stereo) wearing his uniform of jeans and a T-shirt. A super-cautious gatekeeper didn't recognise him and wouldn't let him in so instead of stopping to telephone, Clint just wheeled his truck around and went back home. He was a star now, he felt, and 'after all, I was getting paid for it so I figured what the hell . . .' It was soon straightened out and he returned.

It was his first musical, and, he's since added, his last, but an interesting experience nonetheless. After several weeks of coaching, he was ready to do the two singing numbers allotted him in the picture, *I Talk to the Trees* and *I Still See Eliza*. Admittedly no Howard Keel in the singing department, the results were very much O.K., hitting just the right note of untutored strength that they really call for. Presnel got the biggie, *They Call The Wind Maria*, but Clint was right in there with the rest of the cast on the choruses.

For five months the entire cast and crew was on location in Baker, Oregon – a town about the size of a TV studio. Once again it was the comraderie of the cast that made it palatable. Always as friendly to the crew members as to his fellow stars, Clint and Lee Marvin spent many a long evening together with the crew in what they called the local Gorilla Lounge. The talk got really interesting between the pair when it turned to Don Siegel. Marvin admitted that Siegel virtually discovered him back in 1952 when he cast him as Sheepdip in an Audie Murphy western called *Duel at Silver Creek*. Siegel has since said there was neither a duel nor a silver creek in it, but that was the title of the script and so it stayed. Lee had also starred as the brutal heavy in *The Killers*, the Siegel film Clint had screened before *Coogan's Bluff*, and they naturally got to com-paring notes on their experiences with him.

Jean Seberg, the actress who'd been burned at the stake by the critics after her debut in Otto Preminger's *St. Joan,* was on one of her rare forays into American films after becoming a top star in France with *Breathless*. Glacially beautiful, she spent most of her spare time remaining aloof from the off-screen carryings-on, preferring the quiet of the rented house where she studied her lines, practised her own singing. No fool, Jean, she was in it for the tidy salary she was being paid and though she admirably tackled the part of Elizabeth, the frontier woman with two husbands, her performance wasn't quite gutsy enough for the pivotal role.

Maggie flew in and out on occasional week-ends and all in all, shooting went well, if slowly. Much too slowly for Clint.

Paint Your Wagon is regarded as a failure even though it grossed almost $15 million, putting it right on the top box office list. The reason, obviously, is that like *Cleopatra*, it was awesomely expensive, going way over budget and for all the wrong reasons. People saw it by the millions, especially with Marvin's and Clint's names on the marquees, yet it never fully jelled as a film despite the several near-geniuses in charge. The critics praised Clint, saying he was probably the best ingredient in a production that started out to be a crusty musical soufflé of the Old West but which once in the oven just never did rise. Though beautifully and dramatically photographed in technicolor and panavision, one critic expressed a wish that Clint had directed it. He felt at least there would have been a little action rather than so many numbing sequences extolling the natural beauty of the Northwest. Clint's attitude can best be summed up in an old vaudeville saying – he went on, did his number, and got off – with the loot safely stashed in his production company's back pocket.

It taught him much about how *not* to produce a movie though, reinforcing his own ideas of tight shooting on a feasible budget. He told Rex Reed, 'It was a disaster.' Then added, 'It didn't have to be such an *expensive* disaster. We had Lear jets flying everyone in and out of Oregon, helicopters to take the wives to location for lunch, crews of seven trucks, thousands of extras getting paid for doing nothing, everyone living in ranch houses – $20 million down the drain and most of it doesn't even show on the screen!' Not Clint's way of doing things by a long shot.

Despite what he may think of a picture, Clint has always evinced a professional's desire to help make it successful in any way he can. For *Paint Your Wagon*, his first 'class' picture, he got his first 'class' publicity – on the pages of *Harper's Bazaar* replete with enough props, models and outrageous fashion touches to gladden the heart of any female or *Vogue*-addicted male, for that matter. The opening shot of the article was a colour close-up of Clint clutching a leather coat over his shoulder with his hand carefully wrapped in a diamond-and-gold necklace. Another showed him wearing a black turtleneck with several studded belts flung around his head, hands fashionably slunk into his front pockets. The Man With No Name had been uncomfortably corralled in finery on the magazine cover, but there were plugs aplenty for his films and that was what it was really all about.

Back in Business with Siegel

With *Paint Your Wagon* firmly behind him, Clint turned his full attention to *Two Mules For Sister Sara* which was ready to go into production with Don Siegel at the helm. No Liz Taylor, however. She'd signed up for another project in the meantime, and couldn't summon much enthusiasm for the film after she heard about its long location shooting in a remote corner of Mexico. When she supplied the long list of personal necessities that were a must for her, the producer of the film threw up his hands and pointed out to Clint that they were virtually impossible to provide. Such extravagance just didn't fit in with what Clint wanted to do, so he and Elizabeth agreed to forgo working together this time.

Clint and Siegel talked the casting problem over and came up with Shirley MacLaine. Shirley had just fizzled in *Sweet Charity* (people just weren't in the mood for musicals) and was looking for a change of pace which *Sister Sara* seemed to be. She wasn't too thrilled to hear about the possibly arduous conditions they'd be filming under but gamely agreed, packed a bag, and showed up in Zapa County for the four-month stay.

Now Don Siegel is a man who is used to making movies his way. One unwritten rule he's long been rumoured to have is to get to know his leading ladies well enough to establish a rapport that makes them open and malleable to his ideas when they are in front of the cameras. Shirley MacLaine wasn't having any of it, thank you, and made that perfectly clear from the day she arrived on location. Any 'method' Siegel might want to use on her could stay right in his script book or wherever he kept it, and her independence immediately created a sub-surface tension between them.

Almost immediately she came down with Montezuma's Revenge, that age-old Mexican malady, suffering with many

88

A scene from *Two Mules for Sister Sara*

Two scenes from the 1971 film, *Play Misty for Me*

Opposite: Armed and dangerous in *Dirty Harry*

Clint Eastwood, the director

other members of the company who had the same trouble. A real trouper, Shirley faced the cameras, difficult as it sometimes was. She made it very plain that there would be no delays because of her. She wanted to make the movie and 'get the hell out of here and back to civilisation', so Montezuma or not, she was ready for every camera setup, letter perfect.

For Clint the location trip was another adventure – he loved it. Of the entire company, he was the only one who didn't get ill and credit, he feels, goes to his diet which consisted largely of fresh pineapples and papayas – still two of his favourite foods. He was also pleased with his character, a gritty mercenary who switches from one side of the Mexican Revolution to another as Maximilian's empire crashes down around him. Shirley had top billing and earned every letter of it, but it's Clint's picture in terms of the action. It was a passport back to the kind of man he knew inside and out, and no expense was spared to construct around him a tight, realistic picture with plenty of room for him to act. The literate script gave him a good deal of dialogue, and he acquitted himself well by it. Nothing was stinted in terms of production: an entire village was built for use in the picture and burned down at the climax.

Visitors came to the location but without the lavish accommodations on *Paint Your Wagon*. Shirley's husband, Steve Parker, came for a while as did Sander Vanocur, the news broadcaster. Shirley continued giving Siegel a very cold shoulder. Steve and Shirley had been married for some time, had children, but lived mostly apart. He in Japan, and she in the United States, or wherever else her work took her. It was a wide-open marriage that had once been the talk of Hollywood, but it was basically a stable one, if somewhat unconventional.

To the villagers, the movie crew was like a gold mine suddenly opened up on their main street. Many were used as extras in the film, giving it an authenticity that Central Casting seldom achieves, and they took home with them more money in a day than many of their neighbours did in a month. They were content to let it all go on forever, a sentiment shared by no one else. Siegel's urgency showed in his direction. Playing a whore masquerading as a nun in her attempt to escape the advancing

French Army, Shirley was somewhat miscast. One wonders what Taylor would have done with it. Perhaps her sleek beauty coupled with the outrageousness of the character might have worked better than MacLaine's gamin-like smile and reactions.

Maggie came to Mexico with Clint initially to help get him set up and visit a while, and also, according to some wags, to keep an eye on him. After she left, rumours bounded around Hollywood that Shirley wasn't the only one receiving visitors and that actress Susan St. James had flown in to help Clint learn his lines on the remote location site. But if Maggie heard them, they went in one ear and out the other. Clint's business and everything that went with it were one thing, but she and his son and their home-life were another. As soon as Siegel called his last 'Print it', she knew Clint would be back in his own backyard.

Many people don't know that despite his image, Clint is not a killer of any sort. One scene in *Sara* called for him to kill a rattlesnake that was threatening Shirley. At first he refused to do it. He was eventually talked into it and did what the script required of him. 'It wasn't the happiest thing I ever did. I cut the snake's head off and handed the body to Shirley.' Talk about realism.

When the film was finished and edited, it fell short of Don Siegel's initial expectations. There was no lessening of his enthusiasm for his star though, and for Clint's potential as an actor. Siegel had already taken Clint out of the Old West and placed him in the modern world with *Coogan's Bluff*; with *Sara* he brought him back again with an important if subtle difference – he'd made him act. Critics be damned, he thought, when the reviews didn't give Clint credit for the fantastic job he'd done in Siegel's eyes. The two were already talking about another project, one that was tantalising to Siegel. He had a script called *Beguiled* and he was convinced it could be the best thing Clint had ever done. If he'd changed Eastwood's image at all so far, the changes were only gentle curves compared to the right angles he was planning for their next film. However, one thing Siegel didn't take into consideration was that the bulk of Clint's popularity was based on his rock-hard ability to survive – a quality his fans were far from ready to see dissipate.

Not that they had to worry on that score immediately because Clint's next film *The Warriors* promised to be everything they were used to and more. Directed by Brian G. Hutton, it was another World War II adventure, only a much earthier one than *Where Eagles Dare*, also directed by Hutton. In this one Clint was the big man in a group of soldiers who decided to take personal control of $16 million of Nazi gold bullion stashed near a town their outfit is occupying. The caper, supervised by a general no less, played by Carroll O'Connor in his pre- *All In The Family* days, takes place during a three-day pass. Eastwood is backed up by Donald Sutherland, Don Rickles, Telly Savalas, and four other mismatched G.I.s.

It was a good tight story, more realistic than *Eagles*, but it required still another long location – five months in Yugoslavia. The money was good and the prospects even better so Clint once again set out to do his job. After all, he'd formed Malpaso and paid its people to make the best deals but, hopefully, this would be the last picture he'd have to do for the money alone. After this one, he would call the shots – all of them.

The town the movie crew camped out in was Umag, Yugoslavia, but its inaccessibility didn't keep interviewers from tracking down the man who seemed to be hammerlocking the world's box offices right down to the canvas. One thing he took pains to straighten out was what he thought of the critical lambasting most of his work had received. He attempted to explain his approach to acting. 'To me, talk is cheap,' he told William Wolf. 'Some people think acting is only talking. Some so-called intellectuals like to think acting consists of doing a lot of yelling. Sometimes it is, but not necessarily. Acting is playing moments, not just conversing. When there is something to say, talk is great. But some of the best moments I've played, I've said the least, and often I've worked at cutting down dialogue. The public understands silence but a lot of times this goes over the heads of people who don't realise that it is difficult to play strength on the screen if you rattle on. I like to make an audience use its imagination. A lot depends on what an audience draws along with you, not only character-wise but entertainment-wise.'

And *The Warriors*, or *Kelly's Heroes* as its title was subsequently changed to, was certainly entertaining. At times dangerously so. The special effects on a war picture are naturally more involved than in a period Western because there are more technical considerations to be handled and, therefore, a greater chance of danger to the people who work with them. The man in charge on *Kelly's Heroes* was a German named Karli Baumgartner, and he took his work very seriously.

'It was rough because the special effects man used real dynamite – rather than just cork and black powder. Maybe he was getting even for World War II, I don't know; he just liked big explosions. We had one scene where we were supposed to run out and lie down and a barn was supposed to explode behind us. And Telly Savalas, he didn't want to do it. Brian Hutton, the director, said to me, "What do you think?" And I said "Well I'll do it, but first we ought to ask Karli what he thinks." So I went to Karli and said "What's your opinion of this explosion?" He said, "I don't recommend your being in this stunt because I just don't know." Which I thought was nice, I mean a lot of guys would have said, "Go ahead, it's not me out there." So a couple of stunt guys did it; Baumgartner set it off and, sure enough, the building disintegrated right behind them. They were walking around talking to themselves having hearing problems for days.'

(Clint wasn't always that cautious: on location for *Hang 'Em High* in Las Cruves, New Mexico, he ditched his stunt double for the pivotal scene where, as the target of the lynch mob, he's dragged across the Rio Grande by a horse while he's got a noose around his neck. He said afterwards, 'So I could feel what it was like and what my reaction would be to being dragged across a river on the end of a rope. Then I could play the scene that followed with conviction and feeling.' Producer Leonard Greeman was stunned when he heard about it but never dared confront Clint with it, saying simply, 'He was doing his thing.')

Eastwood's naturally taciturn manner became an obvious butt of Don Rickles' humour – a fact Clint was none too thrilled about.

After a scene was finished in which the stars heeded Clint's yell to 'Take cover!' by scrambling through a field and over a stone wall during a barrage of shellfire, Hutton called out 'Everybody O.K.?' as the smoke settled. 'I've been shot!' Rickles yelled from behind the wall and Hutton, not believing the company's chief heckler, shouted back 'Good'. No Don appeared, just another cry of 'Get my lawyer in California – I'm gonna sue you, Hutton, for every cent you've got. My leg, it's going numb, numb I tell you. I can't feel anything!' Still thinking Rickles was clowning, several of the cast members walked over to where he was hopping around on one leg. 'Oh, my leg, the feeling is going. You'll regret this, Hutton.' Slowly he eased up his trouser leg and the cast fell silent. 'Blood,' he cried, 'I *have* been shot! I told you, Hutton.' At the sight of the wound, a minor one, everybody came running. Everyone but Clint. While the others scuttled around clucking over Rickles, he just ambled up, looked down at the stricken Don, and said, 'Better get Shecky Greene into costume.' Everyone laughed to ease the tension, but Rickles, who only stared at him disbelievingly, finally exploded, 'My God, he doesn't say anything for months and then when he does open his mouth, he has to be funny. That was vicious Eastwood, that was really low.' Spreading his arms to include the whole company, he called 'Look at him, folks, I ask you to look at him. There he is – Mr. Warmth.' The episode wasn't a serious one, but it suggested that Eastwood prefers having the last laugh.

Clint had this to say about *Kelly's Heroes*: 'That film could have been one of the best war movies ever. And it should have been; it had the best script, a good cast, a subtle anti-war message. But somehow everything got lost, the picture got bogged down shooting in Yugoslavia and it ended up as the story of a bunch of American screw-offs in World War II. Some of the key scenes were cut out. I even called Jim Aubrey, then the head of MGM (and also the man who when head of CBS-TV had dumped *Rawhide* while Clint was filming *For A*

Few Dollars More) and said, 'For God's sake, don't run that picture for the critics until Brian has had a chance to do some work on it. You're going to cut off maybe millions of dollars in box office receipts." Aubrey said he'd think it over, but I'm sure when he hung up the phone, he said to himself, "What does this frigging actor know about millions of dollars? Forget it." It was released without further work and critically did bad.'

It was time to make the break. Malpaso had been in good working order for some time now and all the contracts for movies starring Clint had been fulfilled. Don Siegel came to him ready to go with *The Beguiled* and Clint's enthusiasm was never higher. He told Maggie he was through with any front offices except his own and that from now on he'd do things his way. After all, what had he been working so damn hard for if it wasn't independence? He'd seen the power men stumble and fall often enough to know that he was at least equal to them in know-how; and with Siegel directing him, he stepped into the off-beat role of a wounded Union corporal who's found and saved from death by the inmates of a Girl's Seminary during the Civil War.

The Beguiled is a powerhouse of a movie that gives actresses like Geraldine Page and Elizabeth Hartman some respectable material to work with in their roles as the seminary's headmistress and her initially idealistic assistant. Again nothing was spared to make the action realistic and an actual Civil War mansion located outside Baton Rouge, Louisiana, was found and refurbished as the principal set to which the cast and crew travelled for a five-week stay.

Siegel had put a lot of time into readying production – in fact Clint Eastwood pictures were getting to be a way of life for him. While Clint had worked with others since *Coogan's Bluff*, Siegel had not, going from one Eastwood picture to the next. The novel *The Beguiled* by Tomas Cullinan had indeed beguiled Siegel with its blackly comic twists and turns in a genre quite new to him. It is a story of how love – in this case the love of several strait-laced Southern ladies – gets twisted into a sideshow of revenge and ultimate death by a cast of off-beat characters. When the women first stumble across the wounded soldier their reaction is to raise the blue flag in front of the school to alert any passing Confederates that they have a prisoner to hand over. Headmistress Martha Farnsworth (Geraldine Page) is talked out of it by Edwina (Elizabeth Hartman) who feels that since he's wounded already, they should help him recover, giving him over immediately would surely mean his death. Slowly, McBurney (Eastwood) wends his way into the turbulent affections of both women, plus several of the very nubile students, which results in a steamy brew of tangled desires and emotions.

An incapacitated Clint is pitted against forces he's unfamiliar with, and fight though he does, he's the ultimate victim. When Edwina catches him making love to one of the students, after briefly sharing his bed herself, she turns on him and pushes him down a flight of stairs, breaking his leg. Totally at their mercy now, he can't fight when Martha decides to amputate his leg, and after getting him drunk, does so with the help of her girls. When he recovers from the unnecessary operation, he's filled with bitterness against them all, announcing that he'll sleep with any one of them or none depending on what he wants to do. Martha and Edwina decide he has to be eliminated and instruct one of the students (whose pet turtle an enraged McBurney has slammed against a wall and killed) to gather some poison mushrooms for his dinner. As he eats his last supper, McBurney suffers a change of heart, getting more expansive until finally he realises that it's Martha he really cares for after all. But by then it's too late. He dies, leaving the girls and their teachers to sew together a patchwork shroud for his body.

It is a dandy picture filled with the classic strains of movie horror and orchestrated mayhem. It's taken top spot in Siegel's personal affections of all the films he's done but it makes a fatal error by breaking the rule that has accounted for Clint's success – it let him die. He doesn't survive, and in the minds of a public used to seeing him as the ultimate Superman, he was suddenly a failure – no stronger than any other man.

Reviewers were quick to pick up on his acting, praising it as the best he'd ever done – with the exception of Judith Crist who called the whole thing nothing more than a film 'tailored exclusively for sadists and woman-haters'. (Clint's primary audience seldom reads reviews.)

Universal was also heartily pleased with the picture but not quite sure how to put it across to the public. They knew they had a New Eastwood on their hands, but they weren't sure how to sell him to both his millions of diehard fans and, possibly, a whole new audience. Several ad campaigns were started and scrapped – with the line 'Clint Eastwood has never been in a frightening situation' being the most appropriate. Originally set for a class opening in Hollywood, it was pulled after extensive advertising and opened finally on a double bill. Once released it quickly attained almost a cult status for many filmgoers, but never took off as it should have because it was never given a definite direction in which to go.

'It would have been a more successful picture if I hadn't been in it,' Clint has said. 'It was advertised to appeal to the kind of people who were my fans from the action pictures, and they didn't like seeing me play a character who gets his leg cut off, gets emasculated. They wanted a character who could control everything around him. The other people, those who might have liked the film, never came to see it. But it was good for me in a career sense because it did give the few people who saw it a different look at me as a performer.' True, it did, but as a performer in a Gothic horror story which was totally unexpected. Very shortly the lesson of *The Beguiled* was totally assimilated by Clint. 'To me an actor's success comes not from the magnetism of his personality but more from his ability to select material that would be commercial with him in it.'

Once he'd made up his mind that it was time for him to fulfil a long-time ambition to direct a picture, as well as star in it, that's what he went looking for. He found it in a sixty-page story treatment written by Jo Heims. (Clint knew Jo from the old days when she was a secretary trying to get work as a writer.) It was based on a personal experience of a friend of hers and was called *Play Misty For Me.*

The Other Side of
the Viewfinder:
Play Misty for Me

Just as the news that Clint Eastwood was getting ready to star
and direct himself in *Play Misty For Me* got abroad in the
land, a rumour surfaced that instead he was going to re-tread
the Man With No Name in a South African Western. A
company there called Icarus Films had announced that he was
going to star for them in *Three Bullets For A Long Gun* to be
made on location in Pretoria, South Africa. In fact a deal was
almost signed when the company ran into trouble. Their initial
feature, another Western called *Thou Shalt Not Kill*, ran into
difficulties with South Africa's touchy censors, and had to be
withdrawn as too violent. Unfortunately the movie company
had planned on using the profits from the first picture to finance
their second one. Since there were no profits the whole deal
went down the drain.

It was just as well as far as Clint was concerned because the
closer he got to a finished script on *Misty*, the more enthusiastic he was about it. It was put-up-or-shut-up time now that
he'd decided to sit in the director's chair, but he approached it
with the same cautious, tidy thoughtfulness that was characteristic of him. From the very first, he laid his plans carefully
so that once shooting did start, there'd be as few interruptions
or upsets as possible.

It was to be filmed on location in Carmel. The land he was
familiar with, loved, and lived on was now to be his co-star in
the modern-day tale of a guy, much like Eastwood himself in
attitude, who gets enmeshed in a web of jealousy and attempted
murder. Malpaso's main man in the front office, Bob Daley,
was producing it for Universal release. For several years he

and Clint had been formulating *their* system for making a movie – constructing an interlocking group of men, money and energy dedicated to spare, no-fat professionalism. *Misty* was to be their first testing of it. By now Clint's temper had developed to a point at least equal to his million-dollar-a-picture status (usually taken in $50,000 per year instalments with the rest poured back into Malpaso). Suffering through the other people's technical problems had generated an impatience for putting up with any now that he was finally in the driver's seat. (Don Siegel still tells that tale – which Clint now denies – of an on-location incident while doing *Two Mules For Sister Sara* when Clint's horse stepped on his foot so hard that for a moment Siegel thought the animal had broken it. Clint was so mad he hauled off and punched the horse right in the mouth. The result was a contrite horse and one badly aching hand, but the point had been settled in a typical Eastwood one-to-one manner.) Like the character he'd played so often, Clint himself wanted nothing more than to come in, do his job quickly and efficiently, survive and most of all, come out on top of it all.

Clint plays Dave Garland, a disc jockey and small-town celebrity who can also claim a reputation as the local stud. He's unmarried, with slim ties to a steady girl, Tobie (played by Donna Mills), who at the start of the action ups and leaves him for his capriciousness. After he's finished with his late-night show, he stops by his favourite hangout, a bar called the Sardine Factory, to shoot the breeze with Murph the bartender and maybe pick up on some action. It's there he meets Evelyn Draper, a girl he soon realises is the same one who calls him nightly to request a playing of Errol Garner's *Misty*. He picks her up for a one-night stand, no strings for either of them, but soon finds her coming back to him for more, cajoling, threatening and finally trying to kill him for his rejection of her.

As Murph, Clint cast Don Siegel, and since he was shooting the story line in sequence, it was Don's scene that was number one on his first day's schedule. It started out almost as a joke, a good luck charm for both of them, yet they approached that day's work acutely aware of its importance – 'After all, it was the first foot of film that Clint ever directed.' Clint said he thought of Siegel when possible names for the part had been passed around at a production meeting but that 'there was this thing that he'd never acted before. I'm not so dumb though – he called me irresponsible since it was my first day of directing to have an unknown, a non-actor, but I'm not so dumb because in case I had any problems, I had a director right on the set to cull some advice from. He was so nervous though for the few takes that it's just as well I didn't have any problems. I figured that doing this job would give Siegel a better appreciation of actors and that I would get the same of directors.' (Siegel left as soon as his scenes were shot, saying, 'He doesn't need me.')

The budget for the film wasn't big – one million dollars – but that didn't faze Clint. He'd already planned how he'd get the most out of it, just as Siegel himself had done over the years. 'In the old days in Hollywood, people got classified by how much their budget was – if it was a big one, you were a big money director, and if it was a small one, so was your reputation. Don knocked around Hollywood for years making small budget pictures, now being recognised for how good they really are.'

The pivotal role of the psychotic Evelyn Draper went to Jessica Walter, a very talented actress who'd never been able to make the big star jump despite the glowing notices she'd got on her debut in *The Group*. She and Clint were a nice contrast – the vital, pretty woman with the blood red lips attempting to bounce her emotions off the quiet, initially amused man whose only aim is to get laid and get on to something else, preferably his own bed. (Initially Clint had felt his character too virtuous, but after a bit of rewriting, he wasn't). Supporting roles went to veterans like Irene Hervey, John Larch and Jack Ging, and the entire film was shot in four and a half weeks. One rule Clint had learned was that a subtle bit of experimentation could make an important difference in what ended up on film, and as director he checked himself as actor by use of a newly developed film-taping machine from Video West which enabled him to see every scene as soon as it was shot. The action was filmed right where it conceivably happened. On the highways and in the houses and bars of Monterey. There were no studio interiors whatsoever. The hand-picked crew was small and with the equally tight cast, helped create an excitement that added to the film almost as much as the savage beauty of the California Sierras did.

As a director, Clint stood aside willingly to allow Jessica Walter scenes that firmly established her as one of the most vividly talented ladies in the business. Her performance is completely captivating. She changes easily from what she feels is love, to fear, to rejection, to hate and finally revenge, digging deeply into each emotion as she goes. When filming was completed, Clint's work had just begun as he fully intended to supervise every frame of the film to the final cut. Remembering the unheeded advice he'd given MGM's Jim Aubrey about the fate of *Kelly's Heroes*, he dug into the studio space he'd hired for editing and started squinting into the movieola, welding the pieces of his film together into a tough, often horrifying whole.

When *Misty* was in the can to his satisfaction, Clint and Maggie packed up to do some travelling. After a stopover in New York where he told Rex Reed 'On my film we had one dressing-room and the girls and the guys took turns using it. No prima donnas, no protocols. Any mistakes are all mine. That's where the business is going, if you want to protect yourself, you've got to direct your own movie.' He and Maggie journeyed on to Italy. (One interesting game would be a guess as to whether that one dressing-room was the one in Clint's custom-built Condor bus which contains, besides a bedroom, a living area, a bathroom and a kitchen.)

In Italy *The Beguiled* was premiering all over the country, and the welcome Clint received was that of a returning hero. The Italians were happy to note that his superstar status hadn't changed him a whit, including the fact he'd just learned upon landing in Rome: he had been named Number One International Star at the Italian box office. (He was number two behind Paul Newman in the United States poll.)

At Milan's Cinema Misure, the première audience greeted him like an old friend, calling out *niente funghi – niente funghi*, or, no mushrooms for me, thanks, in reference to the climax of *Beguiled*. Clint laughed back at them, holding Maggie's hand tightly and smiling down at her. He'd gone out of his way to be there because he knew it would be appreciated. They had just got off the posh Settebello train after fog had closed Milan's Linate Airport, not permitting them to fly from Rome as had been planned, but there was no fatigue evident, just good humour. Dressed in an outfit high-lighted by tennis shoes and a jacket with a sheepskin collar, he mingled shyly with the chicly dressed first-nighters.

After the film these same expensively dressed people crowded around his car, tapping calmly on the window and smiling '*niente funghi*, Clint', as the pair drove off to the Principe's Savoia Hotel, the classiest place in town.

While none of Clint's movies has ever been thought particularly prizeworthy in América, in Italy it's another story. The Italians are indebted to him for the shot in the arm his *The Man With No Name* gave their movie industry and attempted to show their gratitude by throwing a gala for him at the Cinecitta, Milan's film museum and university. He talked to the students – mostly through an interpreter – and at the end of it was presented with a bronze medallion for his artistic contributions to the Italian film industry. Very fancy words indeed, he thought as he accepted it. It was a proud moment for him, especially coming from the people to whom he felt indebted for discovering him and starting *Fistful* on its golden way.

He took the occasion to tell of some of the backstage business and drama that surrounded the Italian Westerns and *Fistful* in particular. 'There were a lot of hold-ups. Sometimes the crew would walk out and it would have been easier to give up, but I thought of Maggie waiting back at home and thought that I could make good with just one picture. When we made them, there was always trouble about not having enough money to pay the crew. But then,' he added sagely, 'if there *had* been a lot of money, I wouldn't have got the movies to start with. I'd have been at home with Maggie, waiting for the breaks while the parts would have gone to Jimmy Stewart or Robert Mitchum.'

When asked about being the Number One box-office star, he

said it didn't feel especially different from being number twelve or number one hundred-and-twelve for that matter. He added that it was sure a bolster to his ego, and that while he never started out to make the top spot, he was heartily glad he'd worked hard enough to help make it happen. (Once released, his films have had a built-in momentum of their own. United Artists discovered this the year before when, as a filler to a drive-in in Factoria, Washington, they'd sent along the three Leone Westerns plug *Hang 'Em High* for an eight-hour Eastwood binge with the marquee saying simply, Spend A Night With Clint Eastwood. So successful was the experiment – the quadruple bill outgrossed the doubled-up James Bond films Universal Artists was also sending out – they continued in Portland, Oregon; Seattle, Washington; Denver and San Francisco before sending it across the country. A bonus for exhibitors was the fact that all that mayhem obviously triggered other hungers in the audience. (One Seattle theatre reported its concession stand was sold out of everything after the first five hours of opening night – with one and a half movies yet to go!)

It's been Maggie's lot that most of the travelling she's done has somehow been connected with Clint's business, but she doesn't seem to mind. After all the years of their marriage, she knows their real happiness is right at home in their 200-acre backyard. When Clint was asked how it felt to be forty-one, he scowled slightly and replied he didn't know since he was still forty. About being forty, then? 'I feel as though a lot of water has flowed under the bridge. I feel cool, just cool.'

Clinton Eastwood, Sr., died in July 1970 of a stroke at his Pebble Beach, California home not far from Carmel. Clint took it as a basic fact of life, an unavoidable voyage for everybody. The two had remained close over the years, but the senior Eastwoods kept their distance from Hollywood and kept to themselves what they thought that kind of life was like. The closest Clint senior got to participating in 'all that' was just two and a half weeks before his death when Clint and Maggie played host to the first Clint Eastwood Celebrity Tennis Tournament at Pebble Beach. Its sponsor was the Del Monte company, and all proceeds went to the Behavioral Sciences Institute. Tennis buffs – of which Clint and Maggie were a newly enthusiastic duo – like Desi Arnaz, Jr., James Garner, Rosemary and Bob Stack, Lloyd Bridges and his son Beau, Robert Wagner and Efrem Zimbalist had all been a part of it, and it had blossomed into an annual event until 1974 when the Pebble Beach Club decided to drop Clint's yearly option on their courts.

As warmly received as he was and as friendly an audience as he felt himself talking to, Clint was still reticent about revealing his private life to the Italian journalists. 'You can sum it up by saying I live in a small town on the coast of California, called Carmel. I have a son and a wife I'm very proud of. The most Italian thing about my private life is that I have a Ferrari. Then there's a pickup, a motorcycle and a small outboard motor. I ride my motorcycle around the Delmonti Forest and Maggie comes with me.' (Shortly she'd have one of her own when Clint added to the family garage for a total of two 750 Nortons, a 650 Triumph and a 250 Honda.)

Asked if he was taking home any souvenirs he said yes, Sophia Loren. Who for? 'Me, although my son is getting big enough already, he'll enjoy her. He's two and a half years old. Looks a bit like me, a bit like Maggie.' When Maggie was asked her comments on *that*, she just smiled and didn't reply. She knew when Clint was joking. He'd once said he liked a woman who knew her way around a man, when to come close, and when to stay away. After eighteen years, she knew the ground rules. 'I want her to have a life of her own away from me. Just a housewife sitting round would drag me down. Besides, as long as Maggie's got a tennis racket, she's happy.'

Besides tennis, the year 1971 saw them both come closer to the Hollywood community than they'd ever wanted to venture before, and they'd begun indulging in the 'inner circle' fun times the social stars sponsored, usually in the name of charity. Clint stuck to the things he knew best but one exception was in March when he went to Bear Valley, California, a plush ski resort in the old Mother Lode mountains of the high Sierras, for the Benson and Hedges Pro-Am Ski Classic. For two days some of the world's top skiers raced down identical slalom courses, competing against an assortment of Hollywood athletes that included Natalie Wood, Hugh O'Brian, Ron Ely and Janet Leigh. Clint himself hadn't been on skis for eight years, and his first day out he took a nosedive. A notice had been posted listing the celebrities' handicaps, and his name led the list. His second time out he fell twice but both times picked himself up and kept going, finally making it to the finish line to the roar of the crowd. The announcer called out, 'Here he is, folks, the Number One box-office attraction, skiing in a style best described as a closely linked series of recoveries.'

He took the kidding easily and later over a beer in the hospitality room said that people had been watching him just for comic relief. Natalie Wood was a close second on the handicap list and took the precaution of having her coach, Billy Kidd, ski down the course just behind her to check her style – a move that had judges checking their rules book. There wasn't any statute against it though, and she, too, smilingly took her medicine when the announcer kept referring to her as a one-time winner of the Harvard Lampoon's Worst Actress of the Year Award.

Nevertheless Natalie came out a winner when she beat former *Batman* Adam West, but Janet Leigh, who hostessed the event, won the celebrity cup and shouted it was better than an Oscar. Back in the hospitality room, Clint managed to put in a plug for *Play Misty For Me*, saying he'd done everything on it 'but clean the toilet', not failing to add that Jessica Walter was brilliant in it.

When the Italians asked him the same question, though, Clint turned suddenly shy, stammering, 'It's just a project.' Producer Jennings Lang, travelling with Clint and Maggie, spoke up saying, 'Excuse me for saying so, but Clint does a beautiful job of directing. We have just seen the first cut and it's one of the best first cuts of a film I've ever seen. With movies getting different titles in different countries, it ought to be called *The Slasher* in Italy.' 'It was virtually shot in my backyard,' Clint added.

Besides tennis and his motorcycles, his Italian fans wanted

to know what else Clint did in his spare time. 'As a matter of fact, most of my life has been spent in preparing my next project.' An unromantic reply maybe, but a true one. To the people who'd discovered him, Clint wasn't about to present any kind of phony Hollywood image of constant partying and fun. His life had always been spent looking ahead. That naturally triggered the question he was waiting for – what was next on his schedule? His eyes lit up, and he smiled lazily when he answered this one, the shyness completely gone. It was almost as if the new project, one he still had control over, were more intriguing, more real than the one he'd just left back in the Hollywood cutting room. 'It's called *Dirty Harry*,' he replied. 'Don Siegel who did *Beguiled* is directing.' *Dirty Harry?* 'Well it's not that he's dirty, but the jobs he gets involved with are – it's a detective story.' The understatement of the year.

The Man with No Name
Meets Dirty Harry

If Clint Eastwood took the traditional image of the Western hero quantum leaps from its classically respectable metaphor to *The Man With No Name* and the *Paella Trilogy*, he did even more to overturn and perhaps re-define the image of the modern day detective when he tackled Dirty Harry Callahan, the toughest nut on the San Francisco police force.

The character of the mangy officer fitted Clint as well as the sweat-stained serape had done him in earlier years – a fact that Don Siegel sensed and pounced upon from the minute he first read the script. The man who had eased Eastwood into modern times with one long desert trackdown at the opening of *Coogan's Bluff* and then took him back again in *Two Mules For Sister Sara* and *The Beguiled*, now pulled him forward again, much beyond the accepted boundaries of law enforcement routine and into a surrealistic world of violence and sadism. The property had originally been readied for Frank Sinatra – who'd started a few blazes of his own the year before in the gutsy *The Detective*. As a result of an injury to his hand, however, and the subsequent surgery it required, Sinatra was unable to take on a part so crammed with stunts and action.

For the first time Malpaso moved its headquarters from the Universal lot to that of Warner Bros., owner of the property. Producer Don Siegel nailed down preproduction details; shooting locations, permission from the city of San Francisco to use its streets and highways for filming; lining up the right crew; all so that director Don Siegel could work with a minimum of stalls and aggravation.

Even though Sinatra's *Detective* had been a box-office hit, the word was out that cop movies had had it. Both Siegel and

Clint knew better once they'd read *Harry*. Rita Fink's character, Callahan, is the supermacho cop whose gun – a heavy magnum – is a potent symbol of masculinity.

The action centres in and around Clint's home town, and San Francisco is as much the star of the picture as he is. An interesting sidenote is how San Francisco has become a place to which Clint constantly gravitates. *Play Misty For Me* debuted there at their Film Festival around the time of filming *Harry* and one way or another Eastwood was blanketing the town – as if the hometown-boy-who-made-good wanted to make sure there wasn't anybody who didn't know it! All the forgotten classmates, the landlords of his parents' houses, the teachers, the straw bosses of his part-time jobs – all those people had to be told and told again that Clint Eastwood had made it, man.

Siegel's direction on *Harry* is as slick and fast as a stream-lined Greyhound, and the picture speeds immediately into the main story of a sadistic sniper, self-named Scorpio, who personally starts a reign of terror in the streets of the bay city by shooting a girl as she lazily swims in a rooftop pool. Demanding a ransom from the city of $100,000, which he doesn't get, he sets his sights on another victim, a black homosexual, but is scared off by a police helicopter. After another successful killing, Scorpio kidnaps a young girl and buries her alive, telling the mayor she had just enough air to last until an immediate payment of $200,000 is made to him. The money is assigned to Dirty Harry to deliver.

Taking Chico, his new and unwanted partner with him, Harry follows Scorpio's direction to the payoff point in a futile runaround which finally ends in Mount Davidson Park. When Scorpio appears to collect the money and hands over the girl's whereabouts, Harry tries to capture him but succeeds only in stabbing him in the leg. He tracks him to a doctor's office and immediately tries to extract the information from him but uses means which the District Attorney later deems as infringing on the suspect's constitutional rights. Scorpio is free, much to Harry's disgust. The girl is eventually found but it's too late to save her life. Furious, Harry realises that his greatest adversary in doing his work as he sees it, is the law itself. It appears constructed to protect the criminal rather than his victims.

He sets out on a personal vendetta to track down and capture Scorpio, (played by Andy Robinson with knuckle-cracking efficiency) but once again the law looms in his way when the suspect complains to the police department of harassment. Harry realises that all he has to do is bide his time. Before long Scorpio strikes again by hijacking a busload of school children and sends another ransom note to the mayor. This time Callahan refuses to be the delivery boy and instead tracks Scorpio down himself. The final chase scene is one fraught with tension and violence (not to mention danger as Clint insisted on doing the stunt himself) as Harry jumps on to the speeding bus from a railroad bridge, and eventually corners the criminal in an abandoned factory where he finally kills him. Action-packed, the picture could have been a producer's nightmare. However, since the producer was Siegel, he and Clint formed their usual bond of understanding give-and-take.

One of Harry's dirty jobs is talking a would-be suicide down from a sixth-storey window. When the time came for the scene to be shot, Don Siegel was in bed with the flu. Clint took the reins then, directing the night scene in his own style, which included the dangerous stunt of travelling up those six storeys in a fireman's escalator – those turntable ladders that look flimsy even on the ground. Chances are Clint would have directed this sequence anyway since he and Don had already agreed that the shot was a Clintus – one he'd thought up himself. Crew members who'd never worked with the lanky star before got a chance to watch him in action that night with his long, almost elegant hands constantly in motion as he stood with the cameraman, pointing, explaining, questioning – devising the shot where the camera tracks dramatically up into the crisp night air.

Fans, too, got a gander at their favourite movie star, coming up to him with crumpled bits of paper to be signed. When he had the time, Clint talked to each of them, signing and smiling. A small Japanese boy came up with a copy of *Mad* magazine to be autographed, opened to the pages of a cartoon article called

A Fistful of Lasagna – spoofing Clint's Italian character. He laughed when he saw it.

When he's working, though, intent on the camera and the glass-walled image inside it, his patience is short. Once during the long night's filming, he blew his stack at a persistent female fan who wouldn't take no for an answer. So incensed did he become over her continual interruptions that he seized the Magnum used in the film and fired several blank shots over her head. She left for good after that.

One reason for Clint's not wanting to waste a minute was that he had a point to prove. 'The studio allowed six days for this shot,' he said during a 3 a.m. beer break. 'I told them I could shoot it in two. So I'll finish it in one – really stick it in and give it a twist.' Give who a twist? 'Some of those studio people, those men in their black suits sitting at their desks who've been around for a hundred years.' That's who.

Clint wrapped up the scene at five-thirty that morning, exhausted after hours of crane climbing, crawling on the window ledge on his hands and knees, and staging a small fist-fight as he wrestles the jumper inside. The result was a tough, punchy scene; a small complete section of Eastwood by Eastwood that helped round out the total character of Dirty Harry Callahan. As everybody got ready to go home, the sound man, a grizzled veteran of many a movie-set war, said sagely, 'He'll make one hell of a good director. He knows the technical end, and he sets things up with the crew. He gets in good with the guys.'

Getting in with the guys has always been important to Clint because that's where he usually feels the most comfortable. People that he thinks are too smart – like movie critics in general – he avoids, thereby leaving himself open to their sharpest darts. He feels they are primarily in that 'Them that can't, teach', category for which he has no use. When *Play Misty For Me* opened at the San Francisco Film Festival, the generally good reviews surprised him, but they'd picked up on the blunt force of his direction and in doing so proved two things. One was that the original character he'd sketched in so many films – and now used in *Misty* – was indeed a deliberate piece of acting; and two, he was able to expand his conception to accommodate an entire film. Judith Crist didn't like it, but by now that fact only made Clint think he was on target. He realised that perhaps the day she *did* start liking him would also be the day the audience didn't.

With the good reception to *Misty*, Clint and Maggie had a chance to catch their breaths before an entirely new avalanche of controversy started after *Dirty Harry*'s première in December of '71. One thing about Clint is that he's always taken time to appreciate a job well done, especially one he had as much to do with as *Misty*. There's a pause, despite his statements of always working on the next project, when he's open and expansive about his work. He is available to interviewers, interested both in taking credit when it's deserved, and finding out what people didn't like. One of the obvious questions was that since he was such a big star, didn't he continually find himself in *Misty*-like situations? 'Well, you know, women do make plays sometimes, but I guess I'm at an age where I don't allow myself to be vulnerable. The *Misty* sort of thing happened to me when I was very young, twenty-one years old, before I got married. Jealousy isn't confined to any particular age, but most people I know, male or female, who have gone through that *Misty* type of insane jealousy had it happen at a very young age.

'I've never been a jealous person myself. I don't know why. Maybe because my parents' relationship was so secure. And as for Maggie and myself, there's always been a certain respect for the individual in our relationship; we're not one person. She's an individual; I'm an individual, and we're friends. We're a lot of things – lovers, friends, the whole conglomerate – but at the same time I'm not shooting orders at her on where she's supposed to be every five minutes, and I don't expect her to shoot them at me.'

As for his switch from in front of the camera to behind it – 'It took me about a week to get used to it,' but he added modestly, realising perhaps he was sounding a little smart-assed, 'after all, I've had a lot of little practice shots over the years.' *Misty* was the first notch on his directing belt, but if he'd harboured any doubts that it would be his last, they were blown away by the solid reception the picture got – and the very solid money it earned ($5.5 million).

That New Year there were more immediate things to think about. Maggie discovered she was pregnant with their second child, which pleased them both greatly, and *Dirty Harry* had taken off like a rocket. It went into profits in a matter of weeks and after several months had already reached the awesome $10,000,000 gross ranks – an assured blockbuster, the biggest of Clint's career, and Don Siegel's as well. Clint was busy filming a new Western, *Joe Kidd*, in the California Sierras at Lone Pine and in Arizona, but was kept well-informed on the noise Harry Callahan was making at the box office and in the *Letters to the Editor* columns of major newspapers across the country.

Besides his star power in the title role, the film was attracting audiences for other, more frightening, reasons. It blatantly fed on the creeping paranoia of millions of big-city dwellers who were drawn to it and almost unwillingly wallowed in its vigilante message. It was also drawing the counter culture, many of whom viewed the picture as a virtual training film on the tactics, morals and temperaments of the police. Both sides saw their guaranteed veneer of protection being stripped away by Harry and his crew, realising for the first time just how thin a veneer it really was.

The whole question of civilian rights, then simmering like an untended cauldron, got even hotter with *Harry*. Many concerned journalists decried its fascistic attitudes. When Harry literally wrings information out of the wounded Scorpio to his cries of 'I have my rights, too', theatre audiences jumped out of their seats shouting him down.

The message of the film is clear from its first important scene – if the law gives no satisfaction, you have to go it alone and take it into your own hands. (This idea started with a police detective in *Harry* but by the spring of 1974 the same plot featured an ordinary civilian: *Death Wish*, starring Charles Bronson, is about a man arming himself and acting like a one-man vigilante. He sidetracks the law which he feels no longer protects the innocent. It too has been an enormous success.)

There were other dangers in *Dirty Harry* that preyed upon the fears of the general public. Scorpio is flagrantly pictured as a long-haired hippie, obviously gone haywire from too many drugs. (The heavy in *Coogan's Bluff* had the same problem, i.e. *anybody* who takes drugs, and has long hair is probably outside the law.) Callahan is depicted as a straight, hardworking cop with only momentary flashes into his non-professional personality. His job is his life but not for altruistic reasons – he *likes* wielding the power and the magnum that goes with his badge. He won't allow anything, even the law, to stand in the way of what he sees as his duty. A very heavy trip, but one that millions took along with Clint in the picture.

Don Siegel knew what he was doing. Each scene is carefully constructed to inflame the lower middle-class phobias and to toy with its most sacred symbols, like the Constitution and the gun. It is an immoral picture, cracking a reactionary whip whose sting can only intensify mistrust and suspicion at various levels of society. Its message appears to suggest that civilians take the law into their own more effective hands. The question can be raised as to whether this sort of picture and others like *Magnum Force* and *Death Wish*, generate their own disciples – giving them the final push from the supposed fantasy of the screen to the reality of the street. In New York in July of 1974 a man identifying himself as Scorpio, called a radio station, saying he'd just 'killed a fag'. He gave an address where the body could be found. Upon investigation police found a dead man at the address and an alarm went out for the killer who shortly afterwards turned himself in. Coincidental?

Clint Eastwood is not a political man. He figures that first and foremost his duty is to entertain. Still, if it came to choosing sides in real life, he would choose Harry's team. 'My favourite role would probably be *Dirty Harry*. That's the type of thing I like to think I can do as well as, or maybe better than, the next guy. He's very good at his job, and his individualism pays off to some degree. What I liked about playing that character was that he becomes obsessed; he's got to take this killer off the street. I think that appealed to the public.

They say, "Yeah, this guy has to be put out of circulation, even if some police chief says, 'Lay off.' " The general public isn't worried about the rights of the killer; they're just saying get him off the street, don't let him kidnap my child, don't let him kill my daughter. There's a reason for the rights of the accused, and I think it's very important and one of the things that makes our system great. But there are also the rights of the victim. Most people who talk about the rights of the accused have never been victimised; most of them probably never got accosted in an alley. The symbol of justice is the scale, and yet the scale is never balanced; it falls to the left and then it swings too far back to the right.'

Clint also doesn't agree with many people's opinions of the picture and what it was really all about. 'I don't think *Dirty Harry* was a fascist picture at all. It's just the story of one frustrated police officer in a frustrating situation on one particular case. I think that's why police officers were attracted to the film. Most of the films coming out then were extremely anti-cop. They were about the cop on the take, you know. And this was a film that showed the frustrations of the job, but at the same time it wasn't a glorification of police work. Although some police department in the Philippines, I understand, asked for a 16-millimetre print of *Dirty Harry* to use as a training film.'

For many the real climax of *Dirty Harry*, was when a disgusted Callahan, still hamstrung by the laws he feels protect the criminals, rips off his detective's badge and throws it into the bay. Many saw that as a contemporary scene akin to the one at the end of *High Noon* in which Gary Cooper, after his showdown, throws his badge into the dust as a symbol of his disgust. Clint disagrees. 'Cooper asked for support from the town he had served so well, and they ended up crapping on him. But Harry wasn't saying the community as a whole had crapped on him, just the political elements of the city.'

The success of *Dirty Harry* has been good to Don Siegel, too. Many people view it as his masterpiece, even those who also see it as a right wing cheer for the law-and-order boys. Details such as the killer's wearing a belt with a peace symbol buckle on it have provoked much comment from anti-Siegel people, yet Don himself wears a ring with the same etched symbol. Siegel said, 'I used the symbol in *Dirty Harry* with malice aforethought. I don't believe that when people are psychotic killers, and I portray them accurately as such, I am condoning them. Any more than I condone the hard-nosed cop, who in a sense is just as much a killer as the psychotic. But I thought it might be more entertaining if by suggestion I should stimulate the audience into thinking. I was showing one person wearing a peace symbol who happened to be a psychotic killer. That's by no means saying that everybody, including myself, is one. No. As a matter of fact, I'm very anti-war. I wouldn't do a film that was pro-war. I'll do most anything, but I won't do that.'

Since the making of *Dirty Harry*, Siegel and Clint have not worked together. For the time being that picture stands as their mutual masterpiece, social criticisms aside. But that doesn't mean they won't get back together at some future date as Don is still very much a part of the brain trust that helps Malpaso keep making its consistently profitable decisions. But for now Siegel is having a field day. At last he is recognised as a talented and top money-making director. In the past two years he's directed Walter Matthau in *Charley Varrick* and Michael Caine in a thriller called *The Black Windmill* and while these haven't started any flash fires at the box office, they've been well received by both critics and the public. Naturally Eastwood and Siegel cultists are longing for a re-teaming but until that happens, Don can take some satisfaction in retracting a statement he made several years ago when his films were being heralded in Europe but virtually ignored over here – 'I feel like a prophet without honour in my own land.' Siegel now has a stateside reputation as well.

Back in the Saddle:
Joe Kidd *and*
High Plains Drifter

If Don Siegel was responsible for pulling off a new Clint Eastwood with *Dirty Harry*, the result wasn't immediately visible in his next film, *Joe Kidd*. Malpaso Productions had acquired the property from a story by Elmore Leonard called 'Sinola'. They quickly re-named it after the character Eastwood would play, recognising in the script all the essential elements of a Clint Eastwood picture.

Take an isolated Western setting, a conflict between what at first appears to be two wrong sides (thus no need to be moral about the many ensuing shoot-em-ups, of which there are plenty) and add one lone stranger, this time a hunter-guide named Joe Kidd, and you have the basic formula. Luckily, Malpaso got the great Western director John Sturges to put his signature on this one. Sturges had made *The Last Train From Gun Hill* with Kirk Douglas and Anthony Quinn, *The Law and Jake Wade* with Robert Taylor and *The Hour of the Gun*. Sturges himself had done much to create the new Western image of the loner hero, most notably with *The Magnificent Seven*. (In his *The Great Escape* he brought the genre up to modern times, again using actors Bronson, McQueen and James Coburn.)

So *Joe Kidd* was familiar territory for the veteran director and he was in good form for it. Despite some mild ruminations at the beginning on the part of the morally ambiguous hero, the film is primarily a slam-bang, quite mindless enterprise from beginning to end. Robert Duvall plays a cruel, laconic land baron. There is much violence – it clearly carries the mark of a John Sturges Western, though far from his best work as in, say, *Bad Day at Black Rock*.

In Clint, Sturges found a perfect vehicle for his brand of action directing. He made the most of it, switching Joe Kidd first to the side of the landgrabbers (for the money), and then to that of the Mexican Americans trying to hold on to their land. (Does principle rear its ugly head here? No, we soon realise he's chosen them because their side is more challenging than the other, more of a battle.) The spectacular scene at the film's climax when the railroad train is driven off its tracks and right through town is a typical Sturges touch: a barber is shaving an uneasy customer when they hear the loud, unexpected closeness of the locomotive; a drunk in the town saloon looks warily up from his drink, thinking perhaps he's had enough, as the train roars through the side of the building, bringing it down around him.

Clint liked *Joe Kidd* so much he decided to start making plans for another similar picture which he'd both star and direct. It was the ultimate step in his odyssey from respectable TV cowboy to The Man With No Name, to Hollywood's version of him in *Hang 'Em High* and *Joe Kidd*, to, finally, his own version of the character.

As usual Eastwood and Company went shopping for the best. They got it right off the bat in the screenplay turned out by Ernest Tidyman who'd copped an Oscar for *The French Connection*. Tidyman assembled all the bits and pieces of the Eastwood persona and rolled them into *High Plains Drifter*, a tightly packed picture that succeeds all the more due to the care and precision Clint used in putting it together.

It was a family project right from the beginning. Bob Daley of Malpaso, repeated the producing job he'd done on *Play Misty For Me*, Clint's first self-directing attempt, and they put together a tightly budgeted shooting schedule of six weeks, with the entire film to be made on location. Like most of the other people who work frequently with Clint, Bob Daley dates back a while. In fact, they were friends when Clint was first getting set up in Hollywood after his Army years. Over the years they have seen each other's careers develop in separate directions until the time was propitious to come together in Malpaso Productions. Bob, the producer and troubleshooter, complements Eastwood's directing style beautifully. Whatever one may say critically of their results, the films they've done together have (*a*) made money, and (*b*) come in *on* time and *under* budget – two not inconsiderable achievements.

The location for the movie was a place that had never been used before in a film, especially the way Clint visualized it when he first saw the area. On the shore of Lake Mono in Northern California, he had constructed the mythical town of Lago, a typical settlement of the Old West. Its construction took a crew of fifty-six workers and technicians – working a twelve-hour day – some eighteen days to complete. The result was a sensational, realistic setting, a producer's dream of what the old frontier must have looked like. The roaring climax of the film comes when the town is burned down around the ears of its people and its marauders in a striking scene that, obviously, had to be a one-take shot. That gave Clint the opportunity once again to shoot a film in sequence – a rare happening, as most pictures are literally pieced together in the cutting-room from piles of film and dozens of scenes shot out of order and at different times.

The tailor-made lead was unadulterated Eastwood, even to the point of his character's having a scruffy beard and no name. Instead of Sergio Leone calling the shots behind the camera though, it was Clint himself who set the scene up in the viewfinder, got in it, shouted action, performed it, and then ran the results through a videotape machine to judge his multiple efforts. An actor directing himself in a film has a tendency to undercut his own participation in it for simple fear of over-doing. *Misty* had helped Clint overcome this when co-editors told him there wasn't enough of him on film. He didn't have that problem with *Drifter*.

Basically the film is a story of selfish complacency, as frightened and weak townspeople hire the Stranger to ward off three approaching killers who've threatened to burn them out to settle an old debt. Unwilling and unable to help themselves, the townspeople attempt to foist the responsibility for their survival on to him. He turns the tables, takes control of the town – installing a friendly midget as temporary mayor – and tries to organise the slack citizenry into a self-defensive unit. A galvanising scene is the one in which he marshals the feeble forces and names each man a member of his militia, telling them, 'You don't want to get shot. You don't want your shops or your houses burned, you don't want your women touched – you don't want anything to happen except you're afraid to do anything about it, or you don't know how.' Whereupon he teaches them – painstakingly – every trick in his survival pack.

The six-week shooting schedule was met with two days to spare, including the time required for the extensive special effects. Shooting in sequence cut down on the editing time, which was done daily in a log cabin fitted out with a movieola and other necessaries. Clint remarked it was the most pleasant way to edit a movie that he could think of. He had had enough of the sterile concrete cubes used when doing bits of *Misty* at Universal. The mountain air plus the enthusiasm of the star kept up the company's collective adrenalin so that shooting proceeded at a fast clip and scene after scene was shot, cut and canned right on the premises. Clint admits that much of his fast pace while working comes from a desire to get back to Carmel and the solitude of his woods and his family.

The leading woman in *Drifter* was Verna Bloom but, as usual in an Eastwood pic, the woman doesn't get a chance to do more than giggle, taunt and then succumb again and again to the Stranger. To an Eastwood-type hero, women are little more than necessary distractions to be used whenever and *if* ever the hero-loner-killer-mercenary gets a chance – which isn't often, with a schedule like his. To Eastwood's characters, every woman is approachable and ultimately available, a fact that audiences have never bothered to argue with him about. In fact most agree that to see him walk into the sunset with a woman rather than his horse would be laughable.

The reception *High Plains Drifter* got was a mixed one. Audiences loved it, especially hardcore fans who appreciated the subtle moves The Man With No Name had made in the seven years since his American arrival. Coming right on top of

Dirty Harry, however, it laid Clint open to even more criticism concerning the code of violence he seemed to be celebrating in picture after picture. The staid voices of the establishment finally got the message that Eastwood and his films were here to stay and began voicing their opinions on that subject loud and clear. Magazines were using headlines like 'Hollywood's Number One Star and Number One Killer!' Clint was compelled to defend himself as he did on the *Tonight* show – after discreetly showing a scene from a film, of course.

'I don't think *Drifter* is a violent film even though I've been involved in a few that were,' he said. 'It's a comment on what's happening today, with the "I don't want to get involved" syndrome that's passing through the country, and it's about a town that is perfectly willing to accept violence on any terms as long as it doesn't affect them. (They all stood back when the first town marshal had been whipped to death by the three killers.) But it finally does involve them due to the protagonist of the film, which I play, and they're forced to stand up and defend themselves, which they don't do extremely well.'

Another remark he made that night was one which showed where his own head was in relation to the characters he played and the movies he starred in – 'I've been very fortunate in my life to be able to play in Westerns because I've been able to release my fantasies through acting in them.' It was an admission that he felt he *was* The Man With No Name and if anyone had ever thought his fantasies were of the 1930s guitar-strumming, good-guy variety, they realised they'd guessed wrong.

One thing that could have been used to soften his reputation at this time was the birth of his second child on May 23rd, 1972. It was a daughter, and he and Maggie named her Allison, but the idea of making news out of the event never occurred to him.

Never having been a publicity machine-made star, Clint has strong feelings about people who hide their own actions behind a *Daily News* layout of home, hearth and the kiddies. He's been around Hollywood long enough to know first-hand the dangers of being famous. He does not wish his children to suffer in any way because he's their father. There are things he wants to share with them and one is the sense of being able to grow up as an individual, not as a son or a daughter of a movie star.

Clint and Maggie waited fifteen years into their marriage before having their son Kyle and the reason behind that deliberate wait is another part of this theory. The children are an extension of them both and came at a time when they were both ready for them. Clint was thirty-eight years old when his son was born, an age when many men have already had their families and have already seen them start to grow up. But Clint shares some of the old-fashioned values of the characters he often plays on-screen. He's attracted to the times when people thought things out and took responsibility for their actions. 'I think it felt better for me at this age than it would have when I was twenty-one trying to start a career. I wasn't broke like my father was when he had me. I suppose that's the reason we had them late in life. But I think I appreciate kids more now, much more.'

Freed of the anxiety and precariousness of trying to establish a career he can now properly devote whatever time he has to his children with a clear conscience, knowing they know he's with them because he wants to be. When he isn't, as often happens when shooting on location or making long publicity trips to promote a new movie, Maggie steps in as both mom and dad to them, but that, too, is nothing out of the ordinary. If Maggie Eastwood's learned nothing else in her twenty-one years with Clint, she's learned to be flexible.

Clint and Maggie are smart enough to know what can happen to Hollywood youngsters if there isn't the proper balance of supervision, support and basic old-fashioned togetherness. No Beverly Hills day school for Kyle and Allison. Kyle goes to school right in Carmel and Allison will most likely do the same when the time comes. Their parents have both seen too many second-generation Hollywood kids end up on the front pages in a town where *any* 'name' news takes precedence over national affairs. The private clubs of Beverly Hills are the playground for these youngers who've spent their formative years in a second-hand limelight, the glare of which has blinded many to the real values of life. Famous people's children attract fringe people on the Hollywood scene and too often the results of these friendships have been unsavoury news. When Charles Manson was apprehended in the Sharon Tate murders, the names of many of Hollywood's biggest names and second generation names were found among his belongings. Dennis Wilson of the *Beach Boys* and Doris Day's son Terry Melcher, both of whom knew him through his aborted music career, were only two to hit the headlines. The memory of the Lana Turner-Johnny Stompanato scandal in 1958 is another incident Hollywood parents would like to forget. Lana's daughter Cheryl Crane, arrested for Stompanato's murder in defence of her mother, is just another name on a long casualty list. For every Liza Minelli and Jack Haley, Jr., there are tragedies like Diane Linkletter, Art's daughter, who killed herself during a bad drug trip in 1970. For the time being, anyway, the Eastwoods feel insulation is the best way to handle the question of their children and the public. Pictures of the entire family are rare, and it will probably stay that way until much later. While they're young, they want them to be as free and uninhibited as any other children.

Their back-to-nature life in Carmel has other aspects to fortify Clint's image as the last of the rugged individualists. Since it's a remote section with the house situated off to itself on a large area of densely-wooded land, Clint has had to adopt a policy of self-defence that's become increasingly common in America. He frankly admits that if anybody tried to break into his house, 'He'd risk getting shot. Yes, I have guns; but with kids one has to be very intelligent about where one places them. My kids play with toy guns, or my boy does, but I've taken him out to the range where I fire pistols, and I've always instilled in his mind that one kind of gun is a plaything and another is the real thing. There's no use trying to tell him not to have anything to do with guns. You can be an idealist and not buy war toys, but a boy will still pick up a stick and play shoot-'em-up.'

Although he acknowledges he likes guns and shooting as a sport (he practises an hour a day when home in Carmel), Clint is a firm advocate for stricter gun laws than the ones already in existence. Part of the *Dirty Harry* backlash was that the public began to think he might be just the opposite since a gun is as firm a part of his image as the trench coat was to Alan Ladd's and blond hair is to Robert Redford's. But on this question he has firm views. 'All guns should be registered, I don't think legitimate gun owners would mind that kind of legislation. Right now the furore against a gun law is by gun owners who are over-reacting. They're worried that all guns are going to be recalled. It's impossible to take guns out of circulation and that's why firearms should be registered and mail order delivery of guns halted.'

During the height of Clint's publicity flap over *Dirty Harry* and *High Plains Drifter*, it became obvious some people saw him in a different light. In August of 1972, President Richard M. Nixon appointed him to a seven-year seat on the prestigious National Council of the Arts in recognition of his clear and unmistakable contribution to motion pictures and also as a tribute to his huge success with the public. Nixon always liked winners.

Hollywood's Newest
Renaissance Man

Just when people have Clint Eastwood pegged one way, he up and surprises them with a turnabout carefully calculated to keep them on guard as to future predictions. He doesn't like to be pegged as anything but what he is, and what he is changes constantly – sometimes even *his* hot sun of violence cools.

At least it did with *Breezy*, the third film he's directed, but the only one so far that he hasn't also starred in. Many people thought Clint was biting off more than even he could chew this time. He was dealing with a totally different type of film from what he'd ever been involved with before – a contemporary love story. Industry scoffers watched the action with interest as the project took shape but when they heard the plot, they snickered openly in the bars and bistros of Beverly Hills.

Jo Heims, the girl who'd written *Play Misty For Me*, wrote the screenplay of *Breezy* and was signed on as the film's associate producer. Bob Daley was again the producer (as in *Misty* and *Drifter*) and he lined up some other Eastwood veterans as well; Frank Stanley, the cameraman who'd shot both *Misty* and *The Beguiled*; Ferris Webster, the film editor on *Joe Kidd* and *Drifter*; James Alexander, the soundman on *Drifter*; and one of Hollywood's greatest art directors, Alexander Golitzen, an Eastwood veteran from *Kidd*.

Clint decided to remain completely off-screen on *Breezy* for two reasons. One was that after *Misty* and *Drifter*, he realised how difficult it was to do both jobs simultaneously, and the other was, indeed, due to the unfamiliarity of the story line – 'I've never done a love story, so I'm staying behind the camera.' It was a gamble for both him and Universal, the company that, as usual, would release the product. A gamble that both thought worthwhile since the grosses on his two other self-directed films had been extremely good. What they chose to forget was the obvious – his real success with those two films came from his starring in them and would most likely have been equally as successful no matter who did the directing. But Clint's enthusiasm infected everybody around him and the machinery of Malpaso revved up accordingly.

Breezy is a California movie, plugging into the California consciousness as an encounter between the old guard and the counter culture. The action is set in the subterranean Los Angeles where millionaires live only minutes away from the action of Sunset Strip – that haven of all-night grocery stores, neon and run-down bars.

For the male lead part of Frank Harmon, a fiftyish pillar of the establishment, Clint cast William Holden; one of the greatest action stars in Hollywood and a ground-breaking Western star in his own right, as he proved in *The Wild Bunch* (1966), Sam Peckinpah's wild and controversial ode to violence. He and Clint had never worked together before but they had no difficulty in establishing a friendly director/star relationship, particularly since Holden didn't treat Clint like a director, and Clint didn't treat Holden like a star. Said Holden later, 'There has been no temperament, no nothing. I'd forgotten what it is like to make pictures this agreeably. I'll work with Clint any time he asks. Besides he can't pull any crap on me because he's an actor too.'

Again Clint filmed in locales he knew. If Carmel was his real home, Los Angeles had been his first (and still is in part since he retains the Sherman Oaks house he and Maggie bought during the *Rawhide* days) and he knew it like the back of his hand. After all, during the lean years he'd covered a lot of ground between pumping gas and digging swimming pools. It looked like a simple film to shoot, mostly outside shots, on location all around town plus a lot of work to be done at a contemporary house in Encino. In the film it would be Harmon's Laurel Canyon Home.

A simple story, Harmon/Holden meets a seventeen-year-old hippie one night while out walking his dog Sir Lovealot, and, as they say, the sparks fly or at least attempt to. Young Kay

Lenz, a TV veteran of a *Movie of the Week* called *The Week-end Nun,* had been spotted by producer Daley and screen-tested for *Breezy.* She got the title role.

Jo Heims knew much about the Southern California temperament from her years of working there and struggling there before getting a break with *Play Misty For Me.* Unfortunately, that experience didn't guarantee she could pin down as elusive a subject as the fragile story of an ageing businessman and a hippie waif who finagles her way into his life, his bed and, predictably, his heart.

As a director, Clint was facing more than a subject he didn't know – but also a *culture* he was unfamiliar with and one to which his only links on-screen had been heavy-handed put-downs. In *Coogan's Bluff* the man he's hunting is what was then, in 1968, called a hippie. Actually, he was more like a popularised Middle America's idea of one, and the society that he, Ringerman, inhabits is pictured as a sleezy one filled with freaky dropouts. Mrs. Ringerman, the escaped prisoner's mother, beautifully played in the film by the late Betty Field, was an adjunct to this seamy world, covering for him as she did, unable to accept him as anything but a perfect son who once proved it by giving her a set of sterling silver flatware which Coogan immediately put down as 'hot'.) To Coogan the whole culture is a menace, alien and horrifying to his Western law-and-order mind. And in *Dirty Harry* the villain is once again a hippie variant, complete with peace sign and long hair.

In Clint's personal life the underground culture has hardly had a chance to get close to him. He does occasionally acknowledge his debt to the counter culture's partial responsibility for the great wave of fame and popularity that followed the release of *Fistful of Dollars* and its two Spaghetti follow-ups. Unfortunately, this lack of understanding is evident on-screen throughout the film in the many plastic clichés used to indicate Breezy's lifestyle. Eastwood's lack of understanding of his subject matter precluded a believable treatment. Everything was surface – and wrong at that.

In directing Bill Holden in such a role, Clint had a chance to experience firsthand the specific problems of an ageing actor who's made his reputation on virility. During the 1950s, Holden had been the epitome of the masculine star and also of the man of that period – a post-war drifter and opportunist whose personal desires for success gradually dissolve into a simple struggle to survive by whatever means are available to him. In the darkly suspenseful *Sunset Boulevard* (1950) he's frankly for sale as he takes up with fading star Norma Desmond (played by Gloria Swanson in perhaps her greatest role) in order to get a foothold in Hollywood and keep the wolf away from the door. The wolf turns out to be *inside*, however, and he ends up being her ultimate victim, a prop in the swimming pool she uses during her final retreat into insanity. Three years later, in *Stalag 17*, he's an opportunist again in a German prisoner of war camp, compelled to con his way to the top of even that limited totem pole. For his tough portrayal, he won the Best Actor Oscar. In Josh Logan's poignant version of *Picnic* (1955) the handwriting of his character's ultimate failure is written handily on the screen as the film opens with his jumping from a freight train, a still handsome man but one saddled with a precarious despair that oncoming middle-age has forced upon him. As he postures harmlessly before the small-town women, we get flashes of how successful his style must once have been for him, but there's a dead-end quality about him now that even the remnants of his sexuality can't hide. He's just another good-looking guy who thought the free ride would go on forever, or at least until he ran into that elusive big break.

Holden's screen career has had to change greatly in the past few years and even he admits a part like Frank Harmon doesn't come along every day. The time of the much older male star wooing, winning and *keeping* a much younger female and having the public swallow it as a straight love story is past. (A classic example is *Love In The Afternoon* (1957) with Gary Cooper and Audrey Hepburn). Holden took that same plunge with European beauty Capucine in both *The Lion* (1962) and *The Seventh Dawn* (1964). In recent years he's been off screen more than on (with the notable exception of his Emmy-winning portrayal of an ageing police officer on television in 1974), and part of his good humour on Eastwood's set was undoubtedly because he was on it – and on it as star of the picture.

'He's even-tempered, a personality trait not much in evidence among directors. The crew is totally behind him and that really helps things go smoothly.' Holden added later, 'And by the way, the term "dirty old man" is not allowed here,' he smiled. 'It's not that kind of picture.'

In fact, everybody was on such good behaviour that interviewers, looking for a little strife between what they interpreted as Hollywood's old guard and it's newest rebel, went away heartily disappointed. Any stride that might have developed was always kept well out of earshot of the newsmen.

In fact the only incident that was talked about publicly throughout the whole filming was when Clint tried to rent a corner of the property next to the Encino-located house where they were shooting. He wanted it for a wider angle shot and was told by the owner he could use it for $5,000. No fool, and especially not when it comes to money, Clint just juggled his shot around to another angle and told the guy to forget it. When it came time to shoot the scene, a night scene, Clint looked up to see that the owner of the property had lined up his three cars, turned on the headlights, and revved up the engines in an attempt to disrupt the shot. 'I don't understand people like that,' he said afterwards. 'The headlights went right over us and were no problem at all. The running motors weren't picked up by our sound. In the middle of it I sneaked up the hill and looked to see what he was doing. The guy was in his driveway pouring cans of gas into the cars! All he did was use up batteries and gas. I just hope it made him feel better.'

When filming was wrapped up, Clint and editor Ferris Webster disappeared with the film cans and holed up in a room over the Hog's Breath Inn (a restaurant Clint is part-owner of in Carmel, but more on that later) where they cut it and pieced it together. Films are not entirely made in cutting-rooms however and when it opened, several reviews remarked on that. In general, critical opinion was lukewarm about *Breezy* although Clint's direction got a fair share of 'shows signs of promise' comments. The screenplay and the acting fared little better, and yet the film is interesting to Eastwood's fans because it is an indicator of his attitudes towards contemporary society.

But *Breezy* has not quelled Clint's ambition to be Hollywood's newest Renaissance Man – if anything it's only intensified it. Malpaso is constantly on the look-out for properties for him either to star in, direct, or both. They've found another for him in *The Eiger Sanction*, in which he'll again tackle both sides of the camera. He says he spends every spare moment he can find reading the many scripts that are constantly flowing into Malpaso in the hope of finding just the right combination of elements for the next time out. To him the mountain is never scaled – there's always another level to get to, and that's the angle he sees it at. He never looks down, only up.

If he surprised Hollywood by choosing a story like *Breezy* to make his solo directing debut, he momentarily shocked them on a March evening in 1973 when for a few brief moments, he dropped his cool in front of them and the whole world. The occasion was Hollywood's annual back-slapping affair, the Academy Awards, and the only unpredictable event of the evening was Clint's appearance. It was he who got singled out for much press comment the next day after appearing to flub his way through some decidedly inappropriate patter at the opening of the ceremony. Charlton Heston, the man who was to have opened the show, got held up on a freeway ramp and Clint was rushed in by producer Howard Koch to fill in. It had started out as a good night for him. Maggie was looking beautiful and feeling good, having fun getting ready for Hollywood's night of nights. When they were seated next to their friends Burt Reynolds and Dinah Shore, the foursome settled back to enjoy themselves. 'I didn't have a thing to worry about because I didn't have a thing to do until the very end of the show when I was supposed to present the Oscar for Best Picture. Howard Koch, who's normally a very cool, collected type of person comes up to me and his hands were going up and down like a Singer sewing machine and he told me Charlton Heston hadn't shown up. Well I didn't even know he was on the show, so I said, "Yeah so?" Then Howard said Heston was supposed to

Kelly's Heroes,
another war movie,
this time a comedy

Clint as a wounded
Union soldier with
Geraldine Page
as a seminary
headmistress in
The Beguiled

Opposite: The actor
in his personal
favourite *Dirty Harry*

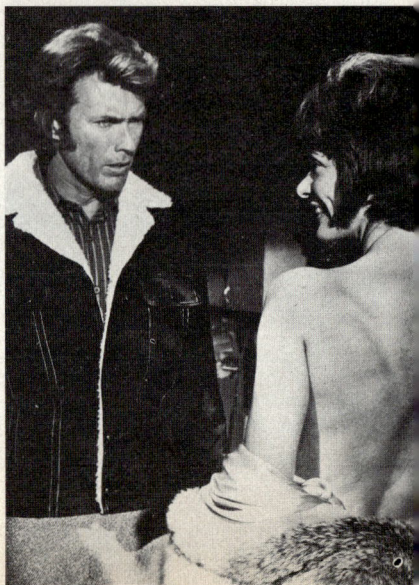

Play Misty for Me.
Clint plays a disc-
jockey, Jessica
Walter an
enamoured fan

Looking rugged and
weathered, in *High
Plains Drifter*

do the whole opening thing and would I come back to do it. I started to say no and look around for Gregory Peck when Maggie nudged me and said to go ahead, you can do it for him, and that's how it happened. He called me backstage and he said, "Here you can do this," and I looked at it and it's all written with these biblical terms – it's written for a man who played Moses, which needless to say I haven't. I said, "Howard, I can't do this, it's absolutely impossible, it's not written for me," but he cut me short and told me to say *anything*, so I took the book and went out.'

Clint's first instinct was absolutely right this time, and when he got out there facing every important person in Hollywood, diamonds twinkling and faces smiling, he froze. Making his way through the teleprompted statements, at one point he became so flustered he said 'Just flip the card – this is not my bag.' Audiences all over the country wondered just what was up with their Number One star. His appearance seemed so greatly out of character and context. He finished by trying to explain what had happened, and added that this was a fine thing to happen to a guy who's only said three words in twelve pictures.

Throughout the episode, Maggie, Burt and Dinah, sitting in the first row, laughed uproariously at his delivery – a fact that he has yet to completely forgive Reynolds for since it was he that egged the girls on. One of his favourite put-downs of Burt is an occasional remark that even though he's not much of an ad-libber, at least he still has all his own hair.

Clint's not exactly noted for his sense of humour – as Don Rickles can testify from their *Kelly's Heroes* days – and being made to look foolish in front of the entire industry wasn't a very simple pill for him to swallow. That night at least, he tried to make the best of it. Koch, appreciating his discomfort, made sure that when he got backstage, sweating profusely and swearing under his breath, there was a cold six-pack of Olympia beer.

Dirty Harry
Rides Again!

One rule Clint Eastwood has learned from his years in Hollywood is that you don't argue with success. When box-office
returns were being added up on *Dirty Harry*, it was obvious
he'd hit the right combination in his role of the scruffy San
Francisco detective. Actually that rule had become almost a
commandment to him as proven by his continual return to
loner Westerns. As successful as they were, and continue to be,
Dirty Harry topped them. On *Variety*'s list of Box Office
Champions for 1974, the picture is easily listed as Eastwood's
largest money-maker to date – almost $16.5 million. At that
time it placed it $2 million ahead of *Paint Your Wagon*, his
musical monument of 1969.

Even before that staggering total was projected by his most
enthusiastic advisers, a sequel to the film was in the works – to
be scripted by Hollywood's new macho-man John Milius, the
gun-obsessed writer who both wrote and produced the most
recent version of *Dillinger*. Predictably the end result was a
wild ride of mayhem, revenge and murder with enough action
to satisfy even the itchiest hardhat, but there was one big
difference: Where *Dirty Harry* portrays a dedicated policeman
out to apprehend a criminal no matter whose civil rights get
bruised in the process, the sequel entitled *Magnum Force* looks
inward, focusing on a group of vigilante cops who have made a
private mission of getting criminals the law has released, in a
carefully planned wave of assassinations.

Based partly on the actual Brazilian Death Squad incident in
1973, the premise was all the more frightening when translated
onto the streets of San Francisco. Co-scripted by Michael
Cimino, he and Milius pulled all the plugs in attempting to

make it every bit as satisfying and as controversial as the original. Controversial it was, but satisfying?

The picture opens with Clint's name competing with a .44 magnum revolver for space on the panavision screen and ultimately the gun is as much the star of the film as he is. Harry Callahan is suddenly wearing a badge again and back on the force (we don't know how he got it out of the San Francisco Bay where he contemptuously threw it at the fade-out of *Dirty Harry*). He is serving time on the routine stakeout division as an obvious consequence of his continuing Dirtiness. When a friend of his appears to be heading for a nervous breakdown, he's concerned since they'd once logged up so many hours together on the force.

When this same friend is killed in an apartment house garage during a routine investigation, Harry takes a special interest in the case. At the same time there's been a wave of murders sweeping the city's underworld; all clean-cut, professional jobs, the victims being gangsters who'd recently been sprung by the law for the usual reason of insufficient evidence and a smart lawyer. The fact that one of these rub-outs happened in the building in which his friend died – and on the same day – leads Harry and the rest of the force to assume the cop surprised the killer during the getaway. Naturally Harry takes it very personally – his friendship is a rare thing and not to be taken lightly – and begins devoting his spare hours to tracking down the murderer. Ballistics reports place the death bullet as one from a magnum, and, as the story unwinds, it becomes painfully obvious to Harry that his friend has been killed by another policeman – part of a death squad designed to take action against criminals who deserved conviction but had beaten the rap. Although no lover of the establishment, Harry is properly aghast. When he is invited to join these élite avengers after confronting them with proof, he refuses, and thereby almost writes his own death warrant. Never fear. Although he's shot, beaten and nearly dynamited, Harry Callahan survives, most likely to surface again in still another sequel.

The interesting thing about the picture is that suddenly

Harry is pictured as an apologist for the Establishment and enemy of the vigilante justice he seemed to embody in *Dirty Harry*. This change of heart doesn't make Harry any the less dirty though, and he's still the same man who feels 'There's nothing wrong with shooting as long as the right people get shot'. In *Magnum* he's the better judge of those 'right people' than are the cops he eventually pursues because at least he claims to support the legal system even though he's all too conscious of its inequities.

Ted Post, the director of *Magnum Force*, directed Clint in *Hang 'Em High*, his first American movie after the Italian trio. Ted found himself once again in the same position he'd been in earlier – that of interpreting another well-established character just as he'd done with The Man With No Name. His view of Eastwood's character in *Magnum Force* was a more physically noble one than Don Diegel had in *Dirty Harry*, and he leaned heavily towards shots that had the camera low and then panning up Clint's long body, making him more monumental than ever. His use of San Francisco as a backdrop for the story was less inspired than had been Siegel's. Where Siegel used the city to suggest a foreboding of the violent fantasies being played out on its street, Post merely used its hills for the now-obligatory chase scenes. (Interestingly enough, Post is considered a good, saleable director, but he seems to be gaining that reputation by specialising in sequels to already proven products, and sequels that don't match the originals for power. Besides the two Eastwood films, he also directed *Beneath The Planet of the Apes* – the least exciting of that successful series.)

Magnum Force was carefully calculated for mass appeal, and there was barely a group it left out in its eagerness to please and horrify. Hardhats liked it because of it's pro-police stance and blacks liked it because, as in *Harry*, Clint again gets stuck with a partner, this time a black one. And the kicker of the story comes when the film's most outspoken liberal turns out to be the leader of the vigilantes. Harry becomes, by default, the most liberal guy around! (Hal Holbrook played the part of Lt. Biggs with his usual authority.)

Top-heavy with brutal action – as in the scene in which a

pimp kills one of his more reluctant ladies by forcing a can of drain opener down her throat, and another where a carload of bad guys is skewered on a forklift derrick – the film gets its message across in the most vivid terms.

In a rare analytical moment, Clint compared the lesson of *Magnum Force* to that which we've been sadly learning from the Watergate break-in and the events surrounding it, particularly the burglarising of Daniel Ellsberg's psychiatrist's office – '*Magnum Force* is all about what happens when the law decides it's above the law. Pretty soon *everybody*'s burglarising. If breaking and entering are considered legal under *any* circumstances, I think pretty soon we'll all just go breaking into a neighbour's house and lift whatever we happen to want or need. Maybe information, maybe his wallet.'

Physically, *Magnum* was a tough picture to make, and Clint got plenty of chances to resurrect the stunt skills he'd moth-balled during *Breezy*. The climax of the picture comes when Harry sets himself up as a target for the vigilantes – or what's left of them by that point – in a chase that goes all over the streets and docks of San Francisco, ending with a motorcycle flight into the Bay. Clint allowed a stunt man to do that last one. The end is in the best tradition of Hollywood – finally it's an individual, an honest cop, who's the real overseer of the law.

The public grabbed on to *Magnum Force* like it's message had been inscribed on stone tablets, pouring $6,871,011 into 401 theatre box offices in it's *first* week of release, instantly making it Clint's fifth most successful picture. Reviews were mixed, but as far as the public was concerned, those writers might well have saved their typewriter ribbons.

Meanwhile, the man whom Clint had eclipsed at the box-office, John Wayne, characteristically tried to come back fighting. With his cowboy movies declining steadily in popularity since his Oscar win for *True Grit* (and, also, many think because of his alienation of many younger fans with the pro-war *Green Berets*), Wayne attempted to steal back his audiences with an Eastwood-*Dirty Harry* imitation called *McQ*. It was released about the same time as *Magnum* and gave movie-goers a chance to decide which of these men was relaying the message people wanted to hear the *way* they wanted to hear it. Comparisons between the two have long been obvious, but this was the clincher. There's no denying the fact that in his time and in the right role, Wayne was for years the prototype of the American hero, and is, when he wants to be, the most ominous force on the screen. He's built his image slowly, painstakingly over the years in picture after picture, from his low-budget Republic Westerns in the Thirties as one of the very popular *Three Mesquiteers* sagebrush series (the other two were Ray Corrigan and Max Terhune), to the classic *Stagecoach* as the Ringo Kid, (1939), to helping win World War II in *Back to Bataan* (1945) and *Sands of Iwo Jima* (1949), then on to open up the West in many Westerns. Perhaps the best of these were Howard Hawks' *Red River* (1948) and John Ford's *She Wore A Yellow Ribbon* (1949). During the Fifties Wayne was the screen's most popular and highly paid star but with his own rah-rah production of *The Alamo* (1960) he began to waver a bit in quality though he virtually owned the Number One popularity spot until Clint took it in 1972.

But he is never *just* ominous and seldom has been as mean-spirited onscreen as the men Eastwood has played. He comes from an older tradition, a throwback to the old definition of the good guy who was indeed tough on the exterior but tender within. Clint had defined a new style of hero – tough exterior and *no* interior. After so many years, playing larger than life heroes, Wayne found it difficult to act mean enough to attract any left-over Eastwood watchers back to his camp. In *McQ*, he's more charming than threatening – especially in his scenes with Coleen Dewhurst – and when he reaches the point where he's supposed to throw *his* badge away, he can't bring himself to do it and winds up having a drink with his arch enemy instead. Currently he's filming *Rooster Cogburn* with Katherine Hepburn, based on the character he won his Oscar for in *True Grit*. There's no doubt there's still a lot of punch left, but it's just getting harder to find the target.

Clint hasn't got the time to worry about anybody's punch except his own, and for his next picture he decided to take, what was for him, another giant step – he decided to talk! And the man he wanted to put words in his mouth was Michael Cimino, the co-scripter of *Magnum Force*. During the filming of *Magnum*, Clint and Cimino had become friendly, especially when Cimino's frequent ideas about the film proved to be good ones. Cimino had shown the same kind of enthusiasm that Clint has for putting a picture together, getting the most out of a phrase of dialogue or a camera set-up; and when the time came to decide who'd *direct* the new project, Cimino got that job, too.

Besides marking Clint's first venture into the heavy dialogue department, *Thunderbolt and Lightfoot* marked another departure for him, it was his first stab at the latest Hollywood box office phenomena, the man-to-man screen team. Paul Newman and Robert Redford had begun the trend with *Butch Cassidy and The Sundance Kid* and were continuing it with *The Sting*. Actually male screen teams had been around ever since the *Boom Town* days of Gable and Spencer Tracy. But where those boys were balanced a bit by Claudette Colbert and Hedy Lamarr in that 1940 hit, the seventies version didn't offer much room for the ladies, and *Thunderbolt* was to be no exception. Clint was teamed with Jeff Bridges, the son of Lloyd Bridges. Jeff is an actor who'd proved himself in *The Last Picture Show*, with a fine performance. In *Thunderbolt* Clint is a tired, and retired thief who thinks his bang-up days are behind him until he hitches up with a young vagrant, Jeff, eager to prove he's just as much a man as his new, initially unwilling partner.

Cimino combined both his visual and dramatic gifts in getting the Eastwood/Bridges partnership off the ground by starting the picture in deceptively quiet style. 'And the leopard shall lie down with the lamb,' reads preacher Clint as the camera pans up the aisle of a starkly simple white church planted in a vast field of waving grain. The leopard is Eastwood and the lamb is Bridges, an ambling rover whom we first meet as he's conning himself a $3,000 used car. The pair get together after Clint's been shot out of his pulpit by a mysterious gunman, and after running across what looks like a five-mile wheat field, comes out on the road where Bridges happens to be speeding along making his getaway. Bridges bumps off the pursuer, and the pair take off together on a ramshackle adventure high-lighted by the narrow escapes, socially comic situations and rinky-dink soundtrack audiences have come to expect from this kind of picture.

It's a fantasy flick, chock-full of all the anti-social actions most people only dream about doing, and enjoy vicariously watching others do on the screen. Lightfoot soon finds out the reason why Thunderbolt Clint was making a run for it across the field. Only *he* knows where a stolen half-million-dollar cache is hidden and which his former partners, in strong performances by George Kennedy and Goeff Lewis, are very much after.

Thunderbolt and Lightfoot lead them a merry chase across fields, through streams, and down mountainsides until Kennedy's car finally collapses and they make their getaway through the soaring scenery of Montana's Big Sky country. One realistic but sadomasochistic touch is thrown in when, after the chase, the boys stop for a breather. Clint has to pull his dislocated shoulder into place, using his belt, which he hitches around a tree and then pulls with his teeth, Gutsy stuff indeed as he stands there bare-chested except for the remnants of his clerical collar. The pair then strike a bargain after Clint painstakingly uses Cimino's dialogue to fill Bridges in on the complicated plot and why he's being chased, deciding to make a grab for the money before the others catch up with them.

When they get to where it had been stashed – behind the blackboard of an old red schoolhouse – they find a spanking new junior high school standing in its place. While that shock's still hitting them, Kennedy and Lewis show up. The four of them then form an uneasy partnership to duplicate the robbery the three older men had pulled off once before. Living in a seedy trailer, they all get local jobs and begin assembling the equipment they'll need, including the surplus howitzer which is used in the climax to blow a hole in the wall of the government vault they're raiding. After much plotting, including Bridges dressing up as a woman to forestall a night-watchman's noticing their break-in, they pull the job off and head for the local drive-in – where Eastwood and Bridges still dressed as a woman, embrace each other as the cops cruise up and down the lines lookng for suspicious cars.

When that ruse doesn't work, they try a getaway with half of Montana's state police chasing them. Lewis is killed and Kennedy, frustrated at being the loser a second time, takes it out on Bridges in a brutal beating scene which leaves Jeff barely able to walk. Kennedy takes the car and screams into a head-on confrontation with the police; ending with his smashing through a department store window – where he's worked as a floor cleaner – and being eaten alive by the store's vicious watchdogs.

But for Eastwood and Bridges, the ending is more romantic. As they hit the highway the next morning, there, in plain sight, sits the red schoolhouse, now a tourist attraction. The money's still there behind the blackboard and they gleefully grab it. By now Bridges is showing evidence of the severity of the beating by a series of nervous twitches, which slow him down. The con and the kid are now rich, and while Bridges waits by the road, Clint goes back into town, cash in hand, and buys him his dream car, a white Cadillac convertible. When he returns and picks up the kid, we know it's only a matter of time, and the picture ends as Bridges crumples into his seat, dead. The camera pans up on the white streak speeding along the highway with its dead man in one corner and a teary-eyed Clint behind the wheel.

Most critics liked the film, commenting on Cimino's crisp way with words and obvious flair for action directing. One of the rawest notices however, came from Rex Reed, who said, among other things, that it was 'a demented exercise in Hollywood hackery', going on to say 'cheap potboilers like this shouldn't be released. They should be recycled and used to catch droppings on the floors of chicken coops.' A potboiler it may have been, following the familiar formula of the Newman–Redford Films and numerous take-offs, but it was also one of the top moneymakers of 1974.

Both of Clint's '74 pictures were contemporary statements, and in both he played obviously stereotyped characters, although completely opposite ones. In *Magnum* he was Super Cop, while in *Thunderbolt*, Michael Cimino paints a picture of a tired man, one who'd already done everything he'd ever set out to do at least twice and now wanted nothing so much as some comfortable peace and quiet. In the first picture he makes the best of the system while in the second he obviously succumbs to its advanced techniques and muscle.

Thunderbolt is especially interesting because it's the first time on-screen that Clint edges away from his reputation as a consistent winner. True, he ends up with all the money, but it's obvious it no longer means much to him, especially since the man he shared the adventure with is now dead. Initially he ridicules the younger man's appetites and in a motel scene early on when Bridges shows up with two eager lovelies and a couple of bottles of bourbon, his lack of interest is written in every line of his face. Even sex has become a chore and the sigh he heaves when the girl gets up off him – in itself a telling power position switch for him – his sigh of relief and exhaustion is long and loud. He overcomes this middle-aged weariness, but that it shows at all is a clue to the reality that Clint Eastwood is growing up.

Just what is it about Clint Eastwood that makes him different from the other male stars of today? I think Michael Cimino knew what he was talking about when, at the opening of *Thunderbolt*, he made the obvious comparison between Clint and the leopard. As Eastwood looks out over the sparse rural congregation, mouthing the biblical words in a sonorous voice we easily sense that *he's* the leopard in the parable – sleek, quick and lethal. He's also the leopard in the particular jungle called Hollywood.

There no doubt that Paul Newman is the ageing king of beasts, a superstar for almost twenty years now since his debut in *The Silver Chalice* in 1954. Still incredibly popular in the right part, as he nears age fifty, his appeal is softened now in contrast to the originally vital glamour that made him an instant star.

Steve McQueen is the bantam rooster, no pretty boy, but with a youthful eagerness coupled with a street-educated sense of awareness that's been honed into a potent screen personality.

Robert Redford is the glamour greyhound of the screen these days after pictures like *The Candidate* and *The Great Gatsby*, whether he likes it or not.

Al Pacino and Dustin Hoffman are the look-a-like puppy-dog types, also necessary heroes in our time.

Marlon Brando remains yesterday's Stanley Kowalski – an ageing bear but it still works, and Ryan O'Neal remains *Peyton Place*'s slightly nasty little rich boy, still unsure of his true emotions, if indeed they exist at all.

But they're all current and potent forces on the screen, all touted as authentic box-office powers and all fully credited in the charisma department, today's word for old-fashioned star quality.

And star quality is exactly what the screen is begging for these days. Movies appear to be returning ever more definitely to the fantasies they started out to be seventy-five years ago. The psychological claptrap and round-heeled verbiage that was slung all over the screen for years is winding down; people want to be entertained again, and to paraphrase Louis B. Mayer, leave the messages to Western Union.

Movie ads for Clint Eastwood pictures usually feature America's favourite phallic symbol, the gun: the magnum in *Magnum Force*, and the threatening howitzer caught between his legs in ads for *Thunderbolt* and *Lightfoot*. It's the country's symbol of manhood and one that has its origins in our not-too-distant past when being a man was more a question of survival than procreation.

It's been said that Clint must have studied at the Mount Rushmore School of Acting and, in a way, that's true. He's attained a monumental quality on-screen – almost as formidable as those carved men – simply by being too big to miss.

Prognosis Positive

Will there be another new Clint Eastwood in the years ahead? Or perhaps more to the point, has there really ever been a new one in the past? Or has the basic Clint simply moved back and forth in time from the gritty spaces of the Old West to the grittier ones he faced in *Dirty Harry* and *Magnum Force*?

Not an easy question to answer, even when one has examined his past and reflected on it. From a distance it appears as calm and as gently monotonous as a patch of farmland from a 727 but which up close takes on the uneven terrain of the earth itself. The public has shown scant remorse in its discarding of Number One box-office favourites, Most Popular Star contest winners, and numerous This Year's Most Promising Newcomers. Often it's because the person has got too old to play himself. But I doubt that Clint Eastwood will fall into that trap. He's an actor who seems to know how to hold on to what he has.

Currently that appears to be just about everything, except perhaps, an Oscar. He's yet to express much interest in one of those anyway. John Wayne never needed one throughout the years of his greatest popularity. Ironically, since he did win one for *True Grit*, it's as if his fans feel he was paid off for the generations of devotion and his career has skidded precipitously with a run of so-so pictures. Another top action star, Errol Flynn, got along very well without an Oscar. It was only his self-destructive lack of discipline that made him come a cropper. His last screen credit was a home movie called *Cuban Rebel Girl* which starred his teenage mistress.

Of Clint's current box office competition, only Paul Newman had really come close to ever winning an Oscar, and after twenty years of top stardom still doesn't have one. Burt Reynolds couldn't care less about one, and Ryan O'Neal doesn't have to worry since the closest he's likely to get is with his *Love Story* nomination. Steve McQueen and Robert Redford are both likely candidates for the honour in years to come, but then there's every likelihood that Clint could make it, too. The vagaries of the nominations and the voting system make it ultimately possible for Mickey Mouse to win another Oscar as he did in the Thirties, but as far as Eastwood is concerned, they can take their time, for all he cares. In fact after the '73 Oscar night incident, he's not even interested in attending the ceremonies any more!

What is most likely is that over the next few years Clint will make more and more of a dent in the director's chair. And that's a prospect that pleases him. (He hates being made up for the cameras and has always maintained that one of the most attractive parts of making the Spaghetti trio was that there wasn't any make-up man *per se* – just a guy with a barrel of phony blood and a big brush to splash it on with.) *Play Misty For Me, High Plains Drifter* and, to a lesser extent, *Breezy*, have proved to both himself and even anti-Eastwoods that he can direct and do it well. Clint looks at a movie as a hungry man would look at a pizza with everything on it – anxious to get right in there and taste all the flavours. He frankly loves moviemaking, every facet of it, and his enthusiasm has infected the people he works with. That same enthusiasm was what forged Malpaso into a tough, viable unit that is the envy of many bigger-monied producers. He brings to his film-making the same toughness he brings to a character he'd play on-screen – the same essence of strength but tempered and heightened by his increasing love for the craft itself.

The Eiger Sanction is the most important film Clint has yet made and plants him firmly at a crossroads. It's unlikely that he'll ever backtrack to The Man With No Name, although it's probable he'll continue doing Westerns as long as the public wants them. The success of his last two movies, *Magnum* and *Thunderbolt*, has made it clear that his audiences are anxious to see him spend more and more time in the twentieth century rather than the nineteenth, and *Eiger Sanction* may mark a new beginning for him.

Based on the best-selling novel by Trevanian, it's a slick thriller that has plenty of action. Clint plays Jonathan Hemlock, a scholarly art teacher/collector who also, as a sideline, is a paid assassin for an underground branch of the state department. It's the first time Clint has interpreted a character who is already identified in the minds of the millions who've read the novel, and it was interesting to see how he handled it. Paul Newman tinkered with the idea of doing it but passed it over, whereupon Malpaso snapped it up. Undoubtedly the character was whittled down some – or up, depending on Clint – to encompass all the trade marks that people expect of him. Much of the film was made on location in the Swiss Alps where the climax of the picture takes place, and true to form, Clint decided to make these sequences as realistic as humanly possible. Before going to the Eiger itself, though, he trained with climber Mike Hoover for three gruelling weeks at Yosemite National Park. The second day there Hoover started earning his salary by giving Clint a large taste of what climbing is all about. 'He took me straight up the face of a vertical cliff a hundred feet high, and then told me to look down. I said, "No way, Mike!" and kept climbing. It wasn't until we actually got to Switzerland on the Eiger itself that I plucked up enough courage to look down at the ground below me. It was terrifying – the adrenalin flows through your body so fast it just seems to drain everything out of you, and your facial expression takes on a haunted look.' When Clint got to Switzerland he noticed that same look on the faces of the professional climbers who surrounded him during the filming.

Unfortunately the realism Clint wanted came with a heavy price tag. On the second day of their five-week shooting stay at Eiger, British climber David Knowles was killed during a rockslide – a common occurrence on what has long been called the Killer Mountain. In fact, its North Face – where the climax of the film takes place – remained invulnerable to all climbers until 1964 when a male/female climbing team finally bested its mile-high, storm-tossed surface. Knowles was killed instantly and Mike Hoover, at his side, was hit by the same rock, but was not seriously hurt. Clint was hanging just a few yards away when it happened and narrowly missed injury himself. 'David was a sweet guy and his death cast a shadow over our schedule and the whole filming. I like to think this film may, in its way, be a tribute to David and all his fellow climbers. They are a breed apart. You form friendships very quickly up there. You have to, because your life is in your partner's hands at all times, and vice versa. The face of a mountain is no place to develop petty dislikes and antagonisms.'

Clint kept Maggie in the dark about his mountainside activities as much as possible, wanting to make the Swiss stay as much like a vacation as possible. That ended quickly. 'Although I knew he was going to do some climbing in the film, it wasn't until I saw the film rushes that I realised what he was doing. I was absolutely petrified at the screening. Clint has always been a very physical person – he likes a challenge. He's the type of man who needs it. I visited the location at the base of the mountain at Kleine Scheidegg, but, when Clint and the crew left the hotel every morning, he used to tell me to go shopping or say it wasn't going to be an interesting day for me to watch. Even if I'd known what he was doing, I know I couldn't have stopped him. Clint is his own man, and I'm glad he is, but I hope that's the last time he'll do anything like this.'

Eastwood paid for the exertion with cuts and bruises – his hands alone took three weeks to heal. He also lost some ten pounds during those rugged weeks, but he was happy, with himself and with what was coiled in the film cans. 'I knew we had to capture the sense of isolation and terror, the chilling feeling of men dwarfed by nature's awesome forces.' Did a press agent write that little speech? Partially perhaps, but primarily it's the declaring of his yearning for realism in an unreal business. It dominates everything he does. He'd bested the mile-high blizzards despite the fears of Maggie and those of producer Bob Daley who gritted his teeth because 'When I saw he was serious about doing his own stunts, there was nothing I could do to stop him – and I knew it.'

No matter how good a job Clint does directing and starring in *Eiger*, and no matter how popular it is with ticket buyers, it's unlikely he'll get Oscar consideration for it. He doesn't play the

Hollywood game and admits it as easily as he admits his taste for beer. He sees an actor's work as going on while the camera's churning, not as launching expensive – and usually unsuccessful – campaigns in the Hollywood trade papers to try and grab Oscar nomination attention to his work. He's only too willing to do the talk-show trail to plug a movie, but as far as getting a grip on Oscar – 'I don't really ever expect to. I'm not going to sit here and say I'd hate to win one. But I'm not terribly politically oriented. I don't know if I'd be able to campaign properly even if I had the vehicle.'

There's a cynicism about winning an Oscar that he shares with Paul Newman, Bob Redford and a few others who've seen the industry machinations that go on when that little yellow telegram arrives saying you're up for an award. Paul Newman's been nominated numerous times for pictures like *The Hustler* and *Hud* but has never been able – or willing – to cop the necessary votes. When Redford got a nomination for *The Candidate*, his only reaction was to add to his Utah barricades and turn the phone off. Hollywood still doesn't like rebels even though they've been their most popular commodity in recent years. Clint said, 'I guess it's possible to win without campaigning but there's definitely a public relations aspect to it.' If he ever is considered for one though, he thinks it might be for Best Director rather than for his acting. And if critics awarded them, he'd never get one.

Over the years Clint has been grist for Judith Crist. In picture after picture she's assailed every aspect of his image, his macho stance and his treatment of women in his films. And women have fared badly, let's face it. In the Spaghetti Westerns they were used and ignored; in *Two Mules For Sister Sara* the only female starts out as an untouchable nun and ends up a whore; the untouchables in *The Beguiled* are quickly transformed into sex-frenzied manipulators, and in *Misty*, Eastwood's magic turns Jessica Walter into an up-front crazy, capable of murder just to get at him. All of which, to Judith Crist at least, has made him *public enemy* number one.

Though Clint is quick to say that critics matter little to him, he once shed a little light on his inner feelings on a TV talk show when subbing host Burt Reynolds asked him who, if he could be any *woman* in the world, would he like to be. He replied he'd like to be a combination of Judith Crist and a seventy-two-year-old prostitute who'd died the week before in a flurry of publicity. Later in the show he took another crack at the question, one of macho Reynolds favourite parlour games, and came up with another combo – Margaret Rutherford and Pauline Kael, another powerhouse movie critic. As usual his reaction to the female of the species was a combination of acceptance of their usefulness and a put-down of their thinking. Whether his answers could be translated into his viewing of Crist as a whorish observer of movies and Kael a humorous one, remains to be seen. The point was not lost on insiders, with the choices perking up quite a few ears, including those of Crist and Kael.

'I face reviews on an instinctive level. I always kind of figure that if they liked the picture, then they're very sensitive, astute and creative human beings, and if they don't, they're bums. It depends on how you're feeling at the moment. They vary from picture to picture. Crist has never liked a picture I've done. In fact, she doesn't even like pictures I'm associated with and not in' – an obvious reference to her dislike of *Breezy*.

'Critics are just like anybody else – they have their opinions and it's very flattering to your ego if they say "Fine, I think this guy did a marvellous job." You see it in print and it pumps you up for a second, but the main thing is how does the public like it. A lot of actors have got too involved in making message pictures, and there's nobody in the theatres to get the message!'

Clint's virtually the last of the million-dollar stars, and, with his production company behind him, he's worked out ways to keep most of it. Malpaso owns or co-owns every film he's in and pays him $50,000 a year for every one of them. His contracts include the most built-in insurance policies for success any star has had in the history of the industry – total control over director, screenplay writer, co-stars, the works. Since he's in the best position of anyone to know exactly what it takes to make an Eastwood Picture after his years in the business, there's not a loose end anywhere that might threaten to unravel the tightly successful structure that surrounds him. His investments are not in blue-chip stocks, but, true to type, in land, lots of it, in California and elsewhere. Of the new show business fortunes, his is estimated to be worth just under the total the Burton's stacked up before they divorced in 1974 and that little pile added up to $25 million on paper alone.

As for those who might wonder if he still delights in the fact that his company has provided his old studio, Universal, with some of their biggest grossing pictures – in light of their dismissal of him in 1954 – the answer is a resounding no. He feels he learned so much there as an extra, salting away the basic information that is the foundation of his success, that their account is settled. His company is based on the huge Universal lot – virtually the last completely intact studio left in Hollywood – but the offices it occupies are modest. Clint knows for sure that fancy offices and many secretaries are just window dressing to the main event.

He also knows that his career hinged largely on a lucky break and even though his Spaghetti-Western style has been widely imitated since the *Dollar* films, it's nonetheless a style more happenstance than calculated. 'Hollywood is a strange place. Everyone is looking for a formula. One year it's two guys on a motorcycle, the next it's a girl dying of cancer, and they flood the market with imitations. For years I bummed around trying to get a job and it was the same old story – my voice was too soft, my teeth needed capping, I squinted too much, I was too tall – all that tearing down of my ego was bound to turn me into either a bastard or a better person.'

And as with any super success story, there are people who support both possibilities. His independence and total self-reliance in a town where active ego building is as much a part of the business as the film that courses through the panavision cameras have made Clint a maverick, an outsider, in the opinion of many. But he's an outsider only because he chooses to be. He has the golden key to every door in his jeans pocket if he ever cares to use it. Nobody's changing the locks on Hollywood's most successful star.

He's come in for his fair share of social criticism from the same people he's ignored. One unimpressed lady in particular was heard to ask 'What could you see in a guy like that? He's so wrapped up in himself. I get the idea that Eastwood would be computer sex. After you look at him, what's left? He's a narcissist – his closest relative is the mirror.' And another member of his female fan club, a columnist, wrote, 'I've never seen a man trying so hard to prove his masculinity – except Warren Beatty. But at least Beatty shows intelligence and tries to be charming.'

Although comments like that roll off his back like rain water off a slippery mule, they obviously haven't given him much encouragement to turn on the charm, which on occasion is quite considerable. While filming *Two Mules For Sister Sara*, there was a rumoured rendezvous in Acapulco with Susan St. James, and even Jean Seberg got a few hints thrown at her by Clint during that long location in Oregon on *Paint Your Wagon*. Yet if it's true, it doesn't make any difference to Maggie Eastwood. She knows he'll always head back to her and the children.

The two of them have formed a solid relationship in their twenty-one years together, and insiders say Maggie's been the deciding factor in his success. So, when rumours on a faraway location start flying around her, she ignores them. But, make no mistake, Maggie Eastwood is no weakling. As a close friend of the couple said in an interview two years ago, 'She's got more steel than a hardware store. Clint talks to her about everything. It's just that Clint likes things done the way he wants them – and Maggie does them that way. He doesn't make a move without Maggie. She reads all the scripts, deals with Clint's agent, and, what's more, she's clever enough to give Clint all the credit.' Even though the pair can now afford any luxury they might possibly want, their tastes remain simple. The hangover of their early lean years together plus the leaner ones of his adolescence have indelibly marked Clint's personality, especially in the cheque-signing department. No matter how much money is in the bank, he knows the only sure thing he has is himself. The example of his struggling parents has instilled in him the lesson that real security comes from inside, not from bank books.

The Eastwood home on Seventeen Mile Drive just outside Carmel is not exactly a second home to their friends, but on the occasion when they do throw it open, it's usually for the old friends they've known and grown with over the years. David Janssen and Burt Reynolds are two of the few from his Universal days. Says Burt, 'They fired Clint because he talked too slow, me because I was incorrigible, and David because his ears were too big. David and I are still doing O.K. and, uh, Clint's not doing bad either.'

Around Carmel, Clint's a familiar sight with very much a 'just one of the guys' attitude. He's been known to stand on line in front of the local movie house with the rest of the crowd, and when he feels the urge, which is often, he'll jump on one of his motorcycles and take off up the coast highway to one of several bars he likes. True, Carmel is one of the richest communities in the world, where other stars like Kim Novak and Jean Arthur are seen doing their grocery shopping, but it's still a shock to tourists to see Clint hanging out at one of the local taverns.

Naturally a guy with his reputation for action gets called on once in a while by men who have imbibed a bit too much and want to prove themselves against the big movie star. 'I don't go anywhere with a big entourage, and I always move out if things look like they're gonna happen. You get bothered once in a while, but most people leave you alone if they see you're busy,' says Clint. Hollywood's full of stories of stars like Bob Mitchum who've given in to the occasional heckler, but Clint's too canny for that. The only headlines he's interested in making are box-office ones. If somebody gets too insistent, and Clint feels the blood starting to boil, 'I usually just get up and split right out the back door.'

The Eastwoods are close pals of Jim and Jane Brolin and the foursome has shared many good times. Jane called Maggie the day she decided to marry Jim Brolin some seven years ago, and Maggie proceeded to set up the ceremony at the Highlands Inn

Chapel in Carmel. After the wedding the Brolins spent the night with the Eastwoods before heading back to Hollywood where Jane was then working as casting director in charge of the *Batman* TV series for 20th Century Fox. Though originally a friend of Clint's, Jane now has much more in common with Maggie. Both women have seen their husbands rise from virtual obscurity to full-fledged stardom. Jim is in the highly successful *Marcus Welby, M.D.* series. More importantly, both have managed to ride the waves surrounding their husbands' successes and stay on board. There are not too many women in Hollywood who can say that, and it's created a bond between them that goes deeper than just friendship. First wives are usually dropped sooner than their husband's first studio options. Over the years it's been a common fate for the girl next door (who married him way back when) to quickly become the divorcée next door – but not in her ex-husband's new neighbourhood. Jim shares Clint's personal lawyer, also the choice of both wives, and Jane takes just as close an interest in Jim's affairs as Maggie does in Clint's.

When Clint and Maggie eat out in Carmel – which isn't all that often – it's usually at the Hog's Breath Inn, a restaurant he's part-owner of. A vegetarian's delight, its menu is loaded with organically grown vegetables and fresh fruits plus tourist tidbits like *Dirty Harry Burgers, Coogan's Bluff Steak*, and *For A Few Dollars More Porterhouse*. It opened in 1972 with several partners. Aside from the no-mistake menu, Clint's occasional appearances there have made it a success of which he's justifiably proud. A natural food buff whose favourite snack is oatmeal cookies, Clint eats there primarily because he likes it. The name of the place can well be called a Clintus since he himself thought of it as a take-off on those fancy names the English give their pubs. Clint got turned on to organic foods when he accompanied a friend to one of Hollywood's many health food stores and overheard what sounded to him like a very intelligent little lecture from the saleslady on pesticides. He admits that natural foods cost more, but in typically Eastwood fashion he adds, 'People who like to save money on marketing will turn around and buy four or five bottles of booze and take them home in the same armload. So I just buy two or three bottles of booze and spend the rest on organic foods.'

Politically Clint is a conservative and typically, it's not a subject he spends a lot of time discussing. He did offer a suggestion on one question, though, when he advocated the legalising of marijuana saying, 'if they legalise pot and put a tax on it, the incoming revenue might cure some more serious crimes than marijuana smoking.'

Clint Eastwood doesn't pretend to have all the answers. Very like *The Man With No Name*, conceived in 1964 on a sand-swept desert in Spain, he's got a set of rules that work for him, and they're the ones he plans on sticking to. He's perfectly satisfied by the way things have worked out, not regretting for a minute the bad times in the past that threatened to keep him hanging in on the bit-part lists indefinitely. 'I was never the guy the press agents figured should be on the cover of this or that magazine, never the recipient of the big, glamorous studio push they gave up-coming actors in the old days. I've never been the darling of any particular group, but somehow – some-how – I got there.'

There is just a hint of disbelief in his voice when he goes over his past and thinks about all the close calls. But the past isn't where it's ever been at for Clint. Tomorrow is the one to think about – because that's the one you have to handle.

FILMOGRAPHY

Filmography

REVENGE OF THE CREATURE, 1955

A Universal-International production. Screenplay by Martin Berkeley from a story by William Alland. Directed by Jack Arnold. Eastwood's debut in a follow up to *The Creature From the Black Lagoon*, and this time the Gill Man gets the 3-D treatment. 82 min.

Clete Ferguson	John Agar
Helen Dobson	Lori Nelson
Joe Hayes	John Bromfield
George Johnson	Robert B. Williams
Lucas	Nestor Paiva
Foster	Grandon Rhodes

(Eastwood appears briefly as a laboratory assistant named Jennings.)

FRANCIS IN THE NAVY, 1955.

A Universal-International production. Screenplay by Devery Freeman based on the Francis character created by David Stern. Directed by Arthur Lubin. Francis the Talking Mule gets drafted into the Navy and is almost sold as surplus. 80 min.

Lt. Peter Stirling	} Donald O'Connor
Slicker Donovan	
Betsy Donovan	Martha Hyer
Murph	Richard Erdman

Commander Hutch	Jim Backus
Jonesy	Clint Eastwood
Lt. Anders	David Janssen
Rick	Martin Milner
Tate	Paul Burke
Voice of Francis	Chill Wills

LADY GODIVA, 1955.

A Universal-International production. Screenplay by Oscar
Brodney and Harry Ruskin. Directed by Arthur Lubin. The
Saxons versus the Normans with the feud temporarily settled
by Lady Godiva's hardly bare ride through the studio back lot.
Technicolor. 89 min.

Lady Godiva	Maureen O'Hara
Lord Leo	George Nader
King Edward	Eduard Franz
Count Eustace	Leslie Bradley
Grimald	Victor McLaglen
Lord Godwin	Torin Thatcher
Harold	Rex Reason
Pendar	Grant Withers

(Eastwood appears as The First Saxon.)

TARANTULA, 1955.

A Universal-International production. Screenplay by Robert
M. Fresco and Martin Berkeley from a story by Fresco and
Jack Arnold. Directed by Jack Arnold. A giant spider stalks the
countryside after being atomically created. The Air Force gets
him. 80 min.

Matt	John Agar
Stephanie	Mara Corday
Professor	Leo. G. Carroll
Sheriff	Nestor Paiva
Lieutenant	Ross Elliot
Old Man	Raymond Bailey

(Eastwood appears as the First Pilot in the plane that bombs the spider.)

NEVER SAY GOODBYE, 1956.

A Universal-International production. Screenplay by Charles Hoffman. Directed by Jerry Hopper. A melodramatic tale of a female amnesiac and the men she can't remember. Technicolor. 96 min.

Dr. Michael Carrington	Rock Hudson
Lisa	Miss Cornell Borchers
Victor	George Sanders
Dr. Bailey	Ray Collins
Dave	David Janssen
Suzy	Shelley Faberes

(Eastwood appears briefly as Will, one of the men in her past.)

THE FIRST TRAVELLING SALESLADY, 1956

An RKO Studios production. Screenplay by Devery Freeman and Stephen Longstreet. Produced and directed by Arthur Lubin. A vehicle for a fading Ginger Rogers as a corset designer who falls for an inventor. Carol Channing's movie debut. Technicolor. 88 min.

| Rose Gillray | Ginger Rogers |
| Charles Masters | Barry Nelson |

Molly Wade	Carol Channing
James Carter	David Brian
Joel Kingdom	James Arness
Jack Rice	Clint Eastwood
Cal	Robert Simon

STAR IN THE DUST, 1956

A Universal-International production. Screenplay by Oscar
Brodney from the novel *Law Man* by Lee Leighton. Directed
by Charles Haas. Sheriff has to fight his townspeople to retain
law and order. Technicolor. 80 min.

Bill Gordon	John Agar
Ellen Ballard	Mamie Van Doren
George Ballard	Leif Erickson
Nellie Mason	Coleen Gray
Orval Jones	James Gleason

(Eastwood appears as a ranchhand in this one with no billing.)

ESCAPADE IN JAPAN, 1957.

An RKO Studios production. Screenplay by Winston Miller.
Directed by Arthur Lubin. Drama about two runaway boys
and their adventures across the Japanese countryside. Released
by Universal International in technicolor and technirama. 92
min.

Mary Saunders	Teresa Wright
Dick Saunders	Cameron Mitchell
Tony Saunders	Jon Provost
Hiko	Roger Nakagawa
Lt. Col Hargrave	Phillip Ober

(Eastwood appears as Dumbo, a screwball pilot who starts the
kids on their journey.)

AMBUSH AT CIMARRON PASS, 1958.

A Regal production for 20th Century Fox. Screenplay by
Richard G. Taylor and John K. Butler. Directed by Jodie Cop-
elan. Post-Civil War Drama about Union soldiers who join up
with some ex-Confederates to squelch the Apaches. Regalscope.
73 min.

Sgt. Matt Blake	Scott Brady
Teresa	Margia Dean
Corbin	Baynes Barron
Corporal Schwitzer	Key Mayor
Private Zach	John Mamler
Private Lasky	Keith Richards
Sam Prescott	Frank Gerstle
Keith Williams	Clint Eastwood

LAFAYETTE ESCADRILLE, 1958.

A Warner Bros. production. Screenplay by A. S. Fleischman.
Directed and produced by William A. Wellman from a story
by Wellman. A romantic drama about the famous flying squad-
ron of World War I. 96 min.

Thad Walker	Tab Hunter
Renee	Etchika Choureau
Bill Wellman	William Wellman Jr.
Tom Hitchcock	Jody McCrea
Red Scanlon	Dennis Devine
Drillmaster	Marcel Dalio
Madam	Veola Vonn

(Eastwood appears, unbilled, as one of the flyers.)

RAWHIDE

CBS Television series, premièred on January 9th, 1959, as an hour-long weekly presentation, it lasted on the air until February 8th, 1966. One of the longest-running series in television history, it was a reliably popular chronicle of a cattle drive in the Old West. It starred Eric Fleming as Gil Favor, the trail boss and Clint Eastwood as his number-one ramrod, Rowdy Yates. (For the final twenty-two episodes of the series, Eastwood assumed top billing and sole star status when Fleming left for a movie career. He died in 1966 while on location for a film in Peru.) Over the years other cast regulars included:

Sheb Wooley	John Ireland
Paul Brinnegar	Raymond St. Jacques
James Murdock	Tom Conway
Steve Reines	Robert Cobal

A FISTFUL OF DOLLARS, 1964.

A Jolly/Constantin/Ocean production for United Artists. Screenplay by Sergio Leone and Duccio Tessari adapted from *Yojimbo* (1961) by Akira Kurosawa and Ryuzo Kikushima. Directed by Sergio Leone. The now classic story of a stranger who rides into an isolated town and pits its feuding families against each other in a battle of which he is the only survivor. Technicolor, techniscope. 96 min.

The Man With No Name	Clint Eastwood
Marisol	Marriane Koch
Ramon Rojo	John Welles
	(Gian Maria Volonte)
John Baxter	W. Lukschy
Esteban Rojo	S. Rupp
Benito Rojo	Antonio Prieto
Silvanito	Jose Calvo

Consuela Baxter	Margherita Lozano
Julian	Daniel Martin
Rubio	Benny Reeves
Chico	Richard Stuyvesant

FOR A FEW DOLLARS MORE, 1965.

A P.E.A./Gonzales/Constantin production for United
Artists. Screenplay by Luciano Vincenzoni and Sergio Leone
from the story *Two Magnificent Rogues*. Directed by Sergio
Leone. Second in the Italian trilogy about two bounty hunters
in the post-Civil War West who track down a sadistic killer.
Technicolor, techniscope. 130 min.

The Man With No name (Il Monco)	Clint Eastwood
The Colonel	Lee Van Cleef
Il Indio	Gian Maria Volonte
Old Man	Jose Egger
Colonel's Sister	Rosemary Dexter
Hotel Manager's Wife	Maria Krup
Hunchback	Klaus Kinski

THE GOOD, THE BAD AND THE UGLY, 1966.

A P.E.A. Production for United Artists. Screenplay by Luciano Vincenzoni and Sergio Leone from a story *The
Magnificent Rogues*. Directed by Sergio Leone. Third part of
the 'paella' trilogy about a trio in search of a tombstone where
a fortune is buried. Technicolor, techniscope. 148 min.

Joe	Clint Eastwood
Tuco	Eli Wallach
Setenza	Lee Van Cleef

with Aldo Guiffre, Mario Brega, Luigi Pistilli, Claudio Scarchelli, Livio Lorenzon, Antonio Castale, Rada Rassimov, Enzo Petito, Sandro Scarchelli and Benito Stefanelli.

THE WITCHES, 1967.

A Dino De Laurentiis Production with United Artists. *A Night Like Any Other* screenplay by Cesare Zavattini, Fabio Carpi and Enzio Muzil. Directed by Vittorio De Sica. A five-part film with each episode having a different director but the same principal star, Sylvana Mangano. Technicolor. 19 min.

Giovanna	Sylvana Mangano
Her husband	Clint Eastwood
Mandrake	Gianno Gori
Diabolique	Paolo Gozina
Gordon	Angelo Santi
Man at Stadium	Velentino Macchi

HANG 'EM HIGH, 1968.

A Leonard Freeman Production for United Artists. Screenplay by Leonard Freeman and Mel Goldberg. Directed by Ted Post. Gritty take-off of the Spaghetti Westerns about an innocent man who's hanged and left for dead but who lives to stalk his killers. Deluxe Colour. 114 min.

Jed Cooper	Clint Eastwood
Rachel	Inger Stevens
Captain Wilson	Ed Begley
Judge Adam Fenton	Pat Hingle
Jennifer	Arlene Golonka

with Charles McGraw, James MacArthur, L.Q. Jones, Alan Hale, Jr., Dennis Hopper, Bruce Dern, Ben Johnson, Ruth White, James Westerfield, Bob Steele, Bert Freed, Todd Andrews and Michael O'Sullivan.

COOGAN'S BLUFF, 1968.

A Universal-Malpaso production. Screenplay by Herman Miller, Dean Riesner and Howard Rodman. An Arizona deputy assaults New York City to extradite an escaped prisoner. Produced and directed by Don Siegel. Technicolor. 94 min.

Coogan	Clint Eastwood
Sheriff McElroy	Lee J. Cobb
Julie	Susan Clark
Liny Raven	Tisha Sterling
Ringerman	Don Stroud
Mrs. Ringerman	Betty Field
Sheriff McCrea	Tom Tully
Millie	Melodie Johnson
Jackson	James Edwards
Running Bear	Rudy Diaz
Pushie	David F. Doyle
Taxi Driver	Louis Zorich
Big Red	Meg Myles
Mrs. Fowler	Marjorie Bennett
Young Hood	Seymour Cassel
Bellboy	John Coe
Omega	Skip Battyn
Wonderful Digby	Albert Popwell
Madison Avenue Man	Conrad Bain
Ferguson	James Gavin
Desk Sergeant	Albert Henderson

WHERE EAGLES DARE, 1969.

A Gershwin/Kastner/MGM production. Screenplay by Alistair MacLean. Directed by Brian Hutton. World War II drama about parachutists who attempt to rescue an Allied officer held captive in a rockbound castle in Germany. Metrocolor, super panavision. 158 min.

Smith	Richard Burton
Lt. Schaffer	Clint Eastwood
Mary	Mary Ure
Turner	Patrick Wymark
Rolland	Michael Hordern
Christianson	Donald Houston
Berkeley	Peter Barkworth

PAINT YOUR WAGON, 1969.

A Lerner/Malpaso/Paramount production. Screenplay by Alan Jay Lerner from an adaptation by Paddy Chayefsky based on the Lerner-Frederick Lowe musical. Directed by Joshua Logan. Musical Western set in the gold rush days about one woman and the two men she's married to. Technicolor, panavision. 169 min.

Ben Rumson	Lee Marvin
Pardner	Clint Eastwood
Elizabeth	Jean Seberg
Rotten Luck Willie	Harve Presnell
Mad Jack Duncan	Ray Walston
Horton Fenty	Tom Ligon
Parson	Alan Dexter
Mr. Fenty	Alan Baxter
Mrs. Fenty	Paula Trueman

KELLY'S HEROES, 1970.

A Katzka/Loeb/MGM production. Screenplay by Troy Kennedy Martin and originally titled *The Warriors*. Directed by Brian Hutton. World War II comedy about a group of soldiers who decide to appropriate $16 million in gold stored in a German town they're occupying. Technicolor, panavision. 144 min.

Private Kelly	Clint Eastwood
Big Joe	Telly Savalas
Crapgame	Don Rickles
Oddball	Donald Sutherland
General Colt	Carroll O'Connor
Moriarty	Gavin MacLeod
Maitland	Hal Buckley
Little Joe	Stuart Margolin
Cowboy	Jeff Morris
Gutowsky	Richard Davalos

TWO MULES FOR SISTER SARA, 1970.

A Malpaso/Sanen/Universal production. Screenplay by Albert Maltz from the story *Two Guns For Sister Sara* by Budd Boetticher. Directed by Don Siegel. A Texas mercenary on his way to Mexico during their Civil War saves a nun being attacked by bandits and later finds out she's a prostitute in disguise. Technicolor, panavision. 114 min

Sara	Shirley MacLaine
Hogan	Clint Eastwood
Colonel Beltran	Manolo Fabregas
General Leclair	Alberto Morin
First American	Armando Silvestre
Second American	John Kelly
French Officer	Pedro Armendariz Jr.
Third American	Enrique Lucero

THE BEGUILED, 1971.

A Malpaso/Universal production. Screenplay by John E. Sherry and Grimes Grice (pseudonyms for Albert Maltz and Irene Kamp) from the novel by Thomas Cullinan. Produced and directed by Don Siegel. A Union soldier seeks refuge in a Southern girls' seminary after being wounded in battle. Technicolor. 105 min.

Corporal John McBurney	Clint Eastwood
Martha Farnsworth	Geraldine Page
Edwina Dabney	Elizabeth Hartman
Carol	Jo Ann Harris
Hallie	Mae Mercer
Amy	Pamelyn Ferdin
Doris	Darleen Carr
Janie	Pattye Mattick
Abigail	Melody Thomas
Lizzie	Peggy Drier
Martha's brother	Patrick Culliton

PLAY MISTY FOR ME, 1971.

A Malpaso production for Universal-International. Screenplay by Jo Heims and Dean Riesner. Directed by Clint Eastwood. Clint as a disc jockey whose life is threatened by an enamoured fan. Technicolor. 95 min.

Dave	Clint Eastwood
Evelyn	Jessica Walter
Tobie	Donna Mills
Sgt. McCallum	John Larch
Frank	Jack Ging
Madge	Irene Hervey
Al Monte	James McEachin

Birdie	Clarice Taylor
Murphy	Don Siegel
Jay Jay	Duke Everts
Man	George Fargo
Locksmith	Mervin W. Frates
Deputy Sheriff	Tim Frawley
Policeman	Otis Kadani
Angelica	Britt Lind
Second Man	Paul E. Lippman
Cab Driver	Jack Kosslyn
Madelyn	Ginna Patterson
Man in Window	Malcolm Moran

DIRTY HARRY, 1971.

A Malpaso-Warner Brothers production. Screenplay Harry Julian Fink, R. M. Fink and Dean Riesner from the story *Dead Right* by the Finks. Directed and produced by Don Siegel. Violent thriller filmed in San Francisco with Eastwood originating the character of Dirty Harry Callahan, a loner cop out to track down a psychotic sniper. Technicolor. 103 min.

Harry Callahan	Clint Eastwood
Bressler	Reni Santoni
Chico	Andy Robinson
Killer	John Larch
Chief	John Mitchum
DeGeorgio	Mae Mercer
Mrs. Russell	Lyn Edgington
Norma	Ruth Kobart
Bus driver	Woodrow Parfey
Mr. Jaffe	Josef Sommer
Rothko	William Paterson
Bannerman	James Nolan
Liquor salesman	Maurice S. Argent

Sid Kleinman	Jo de Winter
Miss Willis	Craig G. Kelly
Mayor	John Vernon

JOE KIDD, 1972.

A Malpaso-Universal Production. Screenplay by Elmore Leonard from the original story *Sinola*. Directed by John Sturges. A relentlessly violent Western with Eastwood as a hunter/guide taking one side then another in a New Mexican land dispute. Technicolor, panavision. 100 min.

Joe Kidd	Clint Eastwood
Frank Harlan	Robert Duvall
Luis	John Saxon
Lamarr	Don Stroud
Helen Sanchez	Stella Garcia
Mingo	James Wainwright
Roy	Paul Koslo
Mitchell	Gregory Walcott
Hotel Manager	Dick Van Patten
Elma	Lynne Marta

HIGH PLAINS DRIFTER, 1973.

A Malpaso-Universal Production. Screenplay by Ernest Tidyman. Directed by Clint Eastwood. A hand-tailored Western designed for The Man With No Name and Eastwood's second time directing himself. The stranger galvanises a feeble town to defend themselves against approaching marauders. Technicolor, panavision. 145 min.

The Stranger	Clint Eastwood
Sarah Belding	Verna Bloom
Callie Travers	Marianna Hill
Dave Drake	Mitchell Ryan
Morgan Allen	Jack Ging
Mayor Hobart	Stefan Gierasch
Lewis Belding	Ted Hartley
Mordecai	Billy Curtis
Stacey Bridges	Geoffrey Lewis
Bill Borders	Scot Walker
Sheriff Sam Shaw	Walter Barnes
Lutie Naylor	Paul Brinegar
Asa Goodwin	Richard Bull
Preacher	Robert Donner
Bootmaker	John Hillerman
Cole Carlin	Anthony James
Barber	William O'Connell
Jake Ross	John Quade
Townswoman	Jane Aull
Dan Carlin	Dan Vadis
Gunsmith	Reid Cruickshanks
Tommy Morris	James Gosa
Saddlemaker	Jack Kosslyn
Fred Short	Russ McCubbin
Mrs. Lake	Belle Mitchell
Warden	John Mitchum
Teamster	Carl C. Pitti
Stableman	Chuck Waters
Marshall Duncan	Buddy Van Horn

BREEZY, 1973.

A Malpaso-Universal Production. Screenplay by Jo Heims.
Directed by Clint Eastwood. A love-affair between an older
man and a hippie girl. 105 min.

Frank Harmon	William Holden
Breezy	Kay Lenz
Bob Henderson	Marj Dusay
Betty	Roger C. Carmel
Paula	Joan Hotchkis
Marcy	Jamie Smith Jackson
Man in car	Norman Bartold
Overnight date	Lynn Borden
Nancy	Shelly Morrison
Bruno	Dennis Olivieri
Charlie	Eugene Peterson
Police officer	Lew Brown
Doctor	Richard Bull
Norman	Johnnie Collins III
Maitre d'	Don Diamond
Veterinarian	Scott Holden
Real estate agent	Sandy Kenyon
Driver	Jack Kosslyn
Waitress	Mary Munday
Saleswoman	Frances Stevenson
Paula's boyfriend	Buck Young
Dress customer	Priscilla Morrill
Sir Love-A-Lot	Earle

MAGNUM FORCE, 1973.

A Universal-Malpaso Production. Screenplay by John Milius and Michael Cimino from a story by John Milius based on characters created by Harry Julian and Rita M. Fink. Directed by Ted Post. Harry Callahan tracks down a team of vigilante policemen in a sequel to *Dirty Harry* – and every bit as violent as the original. Technicolor, panavision. 124 min.

Harry Callahan	Clint Eastwood
Lt. Biggs	Hal Holbrook
Davis	David Soul

Early Smith	Felton Perry
Grimes	Robert Urich
Astrachan	Kip Niven
Sweet	Tim Matheson
Carol McCoy	Christine White

THUNDERBOLT AND LIGHTFOOT, 1974.

A Malpaso Production for United Artists. Screenplay by
Michael Cimino. Directed by Michael Cimino. An ageing thief
teams up with a young drifter to pull a job with his former
partners. Deluxe colour. 104 min.

Thunderbolt	Clint Eastwood
Lightfoot	Jeff Bridges
Red Leary	George Kennedy
Goody	Geoffrey Lewis
Melody	Catherine Bach
Gas station attendant	Dub Taylor

with Garey Busey, Jack Dodson, Gene Elman, Burton Gilliam,
Roy Jenson, Claudia Lennear, Bill McKinney

THE EIGER SANCTION, 1975.

A Malpaso Production, Screenplay by Hal Dresner, Warren B.
Murphy and Rod Whitaker from the novel *The Eiger Sanction*
by Trevanian. Directed by Clint Eastwood. Clint stars as John-
athan Hemlock, art teacher, hired assassin and mountain
climber in a contemporary thriller filmed largely in the Swiss
Alps. Technicolor. 128 min.

Johnathan Hemlock	Clint Eastwood
Ben Bowman	George Kennedy

Jemima Brown	Vonetta McGee
Miles Mellough	Jack Cassidy
Mrs. Montaigne	Heidi Bruhl
Dragon	Thayer David
Freytag	Reiner Schoene
Meyer	Michael Grimm
Montaigne	Jean-Pierre Bernard
George	Brenda Venus
Pope	Gregory Walcott

THE OUTLAW—JOSEY WALES, 1976.

A Malpaso Production for Warner Brothers. Screenplay by Phil Kaufman and Sonia Chernus from the novel *Gone to Texas* by Forrest Carter. Directed by Clint Eastwood. A Civil War vendetta involving guerrillas, renegades and Indians. Deluxe colour. 135 min.

Josey Wales	Clint Eastwood
Lone Watie	Chief Dan George
Laura Lee	Sondra Locke
Terrill	Bill McKinney
Fletcher	John Vernon
Grandma Sarah	Paula Trueman
Jamie	Sam Bottoms
Little Moonlight	Geraldine Keams
Carpetbagger	Woodrow Parfrey

THE ENFORCER, 1977.

Warner Bros. and Warner communications presents a Malpaso Company film. Screenplay by Sterling Silliphant and Dean Reisner. Story by Gail Morgan Hickman and W. S. Schurr. Based on characters created by Harry Julian Fink and R. M.

Fink. Directed by Clint Eastwood. Originally titled *Dirty Harry III*, this actioner continues the exploits of San Francisco police inspector Harry Callahan, this time teamed with a female partner. 97 mins.

Harry Callahan	Clint Eastwood
Lt. Bressler	Harry Guardino
Capt. McKay	Bradford Dillman
Digeorgia	John Mitchum
Bobby Maxwell	DeVeren Bookwalter
The Mayor	John Crawford

And Tyne Daly as Kate Moore.

THE GAUNTLET, 1977.

Warner Bros. and Warner communications presents a Malpaso Company film. Written by Michael Butler and Dennis Shryack. Directed by Clint Eastwood. Clint stars as a disillusioned Phoenix detective given a patsy assignment which involves him and leading lady Sondra Locke in a tense and terrifying obstacle course for survival. 111 mins.

Ben Shockley	Clint Eastwood
Gus Mally	Sondra Locke
Josephson	Pat Hingle
Blakelock	William Prince
Constable	Bill McKinney
Feyderspiel	Michael Cavanaugh
Waitress	Carole Cook
Jail Matron	Mara Corday

EVERY WHICH WAY BUT LOOSE, 1978.

Warner Bros. and Warner communications presents a Malpaso Company film. Directed by Jim Fargo. In this comedy Western satire, Clint plays a truck driver/fighter with a pet orangutan, who travels the Southwest hustling fights.

Philo Beddoe	Clint Eastwood
Lynne Halsey Taylor	Sondra Locke
Ma	Ruth Gordon
Orville Beddoe	Geoff Lewis
Sybil	Joyce Jameson
Echo	Beverly D'Angelo

HARPO MARX

HARPO SPEAKS

I've played piano in a whorehouse. I've smuggled secret papers out of Russia ... I've gambled with Nick the Greek, sat on the floor with Greta Garbo, sparred with Benny Leonard, horsed around with the Prince of Wales, played ping-pong with George Gershwin. George Bernard Shaw has asked me for advice. Oscar Levant has played private concerts for me at a buck a throw. I have golfed with Ben Hogan and Sam Snead. I've basked on the Riviera with Somerset Maugham and Elsa Maxwell. I've been thrown out of the casino at Monte Carlo.

'There are more funny anecdotes in this book than in any other I've read.'

Larry Adler – *Sunday Times*

CORONET BOOKS

THE MOON'S A BALLOON

DAVID NIVEN

He has had one of the most varied lives, as well as one of the most spectacular film careers, of our time. Expelled from school, baptized by the army and a London whore, David amusingly recounts his early adventures.

In America, where he was treated with endearing hospitality, he became a bootlegger, an organizer of Indoor Pony Races, and finally, through a piece of luck which would seem impossible if it were not true, he sailed his way into Hollywood studios and stardom.

His wartime experiences (he served with the legendary 'Phantom') are treated with characteristic modesty; and thereafter his return to Hollywood leads to a rather chequered career (including being fired by Goldwyn and winning an Oscar) and also to the greatest tragedy of his life – the death of his beautiful first wife.

This is one of the most amusing, outspoken, self-revealing, warm-hearted and touching autobiographies ever to be published.

'Delightfully funny. The charm permeates every page'
Evening Standard

CORONET BOOKS

BRING ON THE EMPTY HORSES

DAVID NIVEN

'DAVID NIVEN HAS DONE IT AGAIN!' – *Boston Globe*

Bring On The Empty Horses is a delight from start to finish. With shrewdness and warmth ... Niven brings us Hollywood in its golden prime, from the early '30s to the age of TV. Above all, he brings us *them* – the outstanding stars, producers, directors, writers, tycoons and oddballs, many of whom were his friends ... An inspired mix of descriptions, impressions, and anecdotes. *Publishers Weekly*

'Might easily be the best book ever written about Hollywood.' – *New York Times Book Review*

'Hilariously readable' – *Sunday Telegraph*

'The most amusing raconteur living today' – *Paul Gallico*

Illustrated with delightful snapshots from the author's private collection.

DAVID NIVEN GIFT PACK – is a slip case containing one copy of each of THE MOON'S A BALLOON and BRING ON THE EMPTY HORSES.

CORONET BOOKS

AUTOBIOGRAPHIES AND BIOGRAPHIES
FROM CORONET

ARTHUR ASKEY
☐ 21985 8 Before Your Very Eyes   95p

FREDDIE HANCOCK & DAVID NATHAN
☐ 20513 X Hancock   60p

REX HARRISON
☐ 20651 9 Rex   80p

DAVID NIVEN
☐ 20915 1 Bring On The Empty Horses   95p
☐ 22481 9 David Niven Gift Pack   £2.00

JIMMY SAVILLE, O.B.E.
☐ 19925 3 Love is an Uphill Thing   60p

DENISE ROBINS
☐ 18877 4 Stranger Than Fiction   75p

JAN MORRIS
☐ 19996 2 Conundrum   60p

*All these books are available at your local bookshop or newsagent, or can
be ordered direct from the publisher. Just tick the titles you want and fill in
the form below.*
Prices and availability subject to change without notice.

CORONET BOOKS, P.O. Box 11, Falmouth, Cornwall.

Please send cheque or postal order, and allow the following for postage
and packing:

U.K. – One book 22p plus 10p per copy for each additional book ordered,
up to a maximum of 82p.

B.F.P.O. and EIRE – 22p for the first book plus 10p per copy for the next
6 books, thereafter 4p per book.

OTHER OVERSEAS CUSTOMERS – 30p for the first book and 10p per
copy for each additional book.

Name ....

Address ....

....